RISE AND FIGHT:

Defeat Globalism, Save The West

ALSO BY STEVEN FRANSSEN:

Make Self-Knowledge Great Again

Band Of Visionaries

Journaling For Self-Knowledge

John Rock: Kick Ass, Do Self-Knowledge

RISE AND FIGHT

Defeat Globalism, Save The West

STEVEN FRANSSEN

stevenfranssen.com

twitter.com/stevefranssen

youtube.com/c/stevenfranssen

To all the courageous freedom lovers fighting for Western Civilization.

Acknowledgements

I would like to thank everyone who helped my platform grow in the last year. Your shares and engagement have helped me continue to speak truth to power.

I would also like to thank the friends I have made in private in the last year. Your confidence, insight, and challenges have made me a stronger person.

A mighty thank you to all of the platformers who appear in this book.

Table of Contents

Preface

The past few years since Donald J. Trump declared his candidacy for President of the United States have been an unprecedented time of growth and opportunity for freedom lovers across the globe. His willingness to carry the fight to the media establishment and globalists who run the world has given countless people the courage to contribute to society in a way previously thought unimaginable. Moral people are coming together and rekindling freedom in what has been a decaying landscape of consumerism and nihilism.

This book is my own way of expressing gratitude to the great men and women who have put their entire lives on the line to try and wrestle Western Civilization out of the death grip placed on her. I have paid careful attention to what these people are doing and more specifically, *how* they have been doing it. I have also taken a broad survey of the changing political, social, and moral landscape in order to try and provide context to why these people are doing what they are doing.

The first half of the book delineates the "Rise" portion of the title. These essays focus on how a person can train, prepare, and organize their way into the fight for Western Civilization. The more "sorted out" a person is in anticipation of the fight, the more their training will serve them when bets are off and the masks come down. These essays are of an epistemological nature, laying out terms, principles, and definitions that will come in handy later on in the book.

The second half of the book, "Fight", begins with a delineation of what the "out-groups" are. Our opponents are viewed more closely, including the tactics they employ and what characteristics mark them and rally them together. Also discussed are potential pitfalls and enemies-within that will derail and undermine your ability to be the best culture warrior you can be.

At various points in this book, in-group cohesion will be discussed. Themes within this purview may repeat at a couple points, but from different angles. This is an all-or-nothing information war that will lead to prosperity and freedom or apathy and mass death. Waging the war is not a solo venture. We need good companions and brothers at arms. Collaborating with others is essential. It is in this spirit that several mini-interviews with some of the people I have collaborated with over the years will be included in this book. These are people who have fought in the public sphere for our Western tradition of free speech, the Faustian spirit, and meritocracy. They honor me with their presence and I am grateful for their contributions.

We live in a will to power society. Whoever wants it the most and exercises the most power will be the victor. I would prefer to live in a principled, polite society but globalists and two catastrophic World Wars tore all of that down. Our power does not necessarily have to derive from the political suppression of our enemies, as the Left's does. My contention is that we can wield sufficient power through the argument and through our ability to influence people. We can help people to choose healthy nationalism over unhealthy globalism. Should the argument fail, certain measures to wrestle power away from totalitarian socialists may be necessary. That time is not upon us yet and if this book and others like it are effective, that time will never be upon us. Let's see what kinds of responsibilities we can take on so that freedom will reign supreme and Western man can get on and get going to where he belongs: the stars.

RISE

Rising in the Hierarchy

We need the cream to rise to the top. Through encouragement and speaking the truth from public platforms, we spark whatever latent capabilities, passions, and efforts within the hearts of culture warriors, young and old. This culture war is a Wild West of persuasion and argumentation: an incredible opportunity to rise rapidly in the ranks of society. A new order is being established, one where merit is the bottom line. Now is the time to rise up and help the world.

Let's start first by giving a brief treatment to what will *not* help you to rise in the hierarchy of merit on the side of good in this culture war. Consequently, these behaviors will help you descend into corruption. I'll list three:

Undermining –

Undermining occurs when you convey, at some level, that a person who holds a higher position than you in the hierarchy is fundamentally unworthy and should be held at bay, ostracized, or disavowed *and* you are mistaken in that the punishment does not fit the crime.

For example, some figures on the Right have been involved in doxxing efforts against people who have realistic positions on demographics and intelligence. In the minds of these doxxers, they are fighting against racism and bullying. Philosophically, these doxxers are acting as psychological abusers by disallowing the dissemination of important ideas that will change the political discourse of the West toward a more honest direction. However, these doxxers hold prominent positions of power, through media attention and efforts to "redpill" the public. If we attack them for spurious, unrelated charges, we are undermining them. If we attack, confront, or hold boundaries with them for being psychological abusers because of their doxxing, we are performing an important service to the hierarchy and to the truth.

It is worth noting that power players in the culture war larger than the doxxers themselves may hold some kind of tolerance toward doxxing and thus it would not serve us in rising in the hierarchy to choosing the doxxing behavior of another culture warrior as an absolute hill to die on. Nobody said war was pure.

Another, less abstract form of undermining occurs through nitpicking. Nobody is here to validate that you know such and such factoid better than someone who has a larger platform than you who didn't get their facts perfectly straight. You appear weak to people higher in the hierarchy when you leave a YouTube comment lasting 500 words, setting straight a culture warrior on the actual death count of some far-flung conflict 250 years ago. Stop it. Just stop. You need to deal in principles, not Bill Nye public school perfectionism. We'll cover this more, later in the book.

Being a degenerate –

Self-knowledge affords us a chance to transcend our histories and become someone greater. Degeneracy gains us the easy release of apathy and cynicism.

Broadly defined, degeneracy is any socially destructive behavior.

Drugs distort our perception of reality. They cake our brain with chemicals that convince us we are more functional than we are. We turn away from resolving our personal issues through introspection and into the easy "yes" of brain modification. Personal transformation for the good cannot and will not ever be attained through substances. We must reason and empathize our way out of our denial.

Corrupting the youth can be the hardest degeneracy to trace. People are not yet attuned, on the whole, to be sensitive to the telltale signs of abuse children display. Our societies are still quite numb to the needs and pains of children. We in the culture war are astonished by the images of sexualized young boys at gay pride parades, acting like drag queen princesses and sharing lip kisses with full grown, gay men. This corruption of the youth is toward the extreme end. At the gentler end is the choice to turn a child into a dependent on sugar or the television because these make for temporary, imperfect babysitters of lively children. Sending a child to public school to be indoctrinated in socialism is somewhere in the middle. Much of this is lost on people. We need to point these things out.

One more form of degeneracy is found in post-modernist art. This is art that denies meaning and purpose. It is gutter tripe. Academia, corporate music and video, and government are the primary movers of this numbing, decidedly unsubversive, uninspired movement.

It may gain you an appearance in a Manhattan art gallery to collect 200 gallons of urine[1] in protest of

Donald Trump, but really all you've done is make an ass out of yourself and deny yourself any meaningful employment for an indeterminate period of time.

You can be like Lady Gaga, with all the fame and access to former Presidents in the world, and tickle Satan's fancies in your performances, but all you've managed to do is enslave yourself to metaphorical witchcraft as a concubine.

One more: you may worship at the altar of multiculturalism by supporting "art" that espouses the mixing of cultures as an ideal to be attained. The truth is that there are genuine, important differences between cultures and peoples that cannot be covered up with sitcom shock. It does not make you an "enlightened" individual to applaud scripts crafted by globalist Hollywood writers that are obsessed with ruining everyone's fun. It makes you a tool for the Establishment.

Being a flake –

Comedy films are filled with the trope of the person who doesn't come through when he's being counted on. The stakes are artificial and silly and so the joke works. This book deals with real life. The culture

---

[1]https://www.timeout.com/newyork/blog/200-gallons-of-urine-will-be-the-centerpiece-of-a-new-soho-art-exhibition-081517

war is a war for the soul of civilization. The stakes are sky high, everlasting, and at the core of society. If you make a habit out of inconsistency, you will earn a reputation as "the guy who doesn't show up". You must keep or alter your appointments in a timely manner.

Let's go back over that list and name the opposites. These will help you ascend the hierarchy of good:

Encouragement (Opposite: undermining) –

Encouragement is another theme in this book that will be hammered home, again and again. It is so absolutely crucial that we culture warriors encourage one another. Encouragement literally means "to give courage". If undermining is to pull people down with dishonesty, encouragement is to build people up with honesty. The world is too filled with cynicism, negging, and sarcasm.

Stefan Molyneux said to me once in 2010 that we must be just as wary of praise as we are wary of criticism. What he meant at the time is that you don't want to build yourself up through grandiosity, praising yourself and allowing yourself to be praised for that which is not accurate to reality. How "special" you are is truly of no consequence to the outcome of the culture war. Only your results matter. We are in a dire fight and egos have to be pushed aside.

Therefore, to encourage those above, beside, and below you in the hierarchy means to give energy that plugs people "back into the fight". Those who encourage us the most generally command the field. I am talking about the Molyneuxs, the Alex Joneses, the Donald Trumps, and so forth. They have no time or energy to undermine their allies. They are not doling out unnecessary praise. They are not pulling people into "specialness bubbles". They are plugging people *directly* into the action, the war for the soul of civilization. They do this at a mass scale with polished mastery.

Can you give an enthralling, fiery speech loaded with conviction and truth? Can you wade into the breach like a berserker eyeing Valhalla while keeping your wits about you? Do you know the sweet taste of victory on the battlefield as your leftist enemy crumples beneath your figurative broadsword? Have you seen an innocent person exhaling in relief as you swept them from the throes of danger? Things are getting epic, eh?

Those who convey these divine moments to us with their words and energy are the philosopher kings. They are powerhouses loaded with the spark of human life. They light the way and they show us where we will gain ground. You can practice their art at whatever level you are at.

Here are some small to large practical examples of encouragement:

-Telling yourself you can go to the gym today and then following through.

-Helping a child to learn something.

-Showing a friend you care about their health choices.

-Steering a business toward ethical profitability through your persuasion skills.

-Reaching thousands of people through YouTube with a presentation that counters mainstream media narratives.

-Alex Jones' "The Justin Beiber Rant"[2]

-Donald Trump telling Hillary Clinton "because you'd be in jail" as civilization hung by a thread[3]

Being wholesome (Opposite: being a degenerate) –

Wholesomeness is the quality of being healthy across the spectrum. This includes the mental, emotional, spiritual or philosophical, physical, artistic,

---

[2]https://www.youtube.com/watch?v=n8WhT9BwpRs
[3]https://www.youtube.com/watch?v=AFGiZT-MnI4

and social realms of health. Through self-knowledge according to rationally consistent principles (see my book *Make Self-Knowledge Great Again*), we are able to discover for ourselves how we will embody this quality of wholesomeness. I will give you my perspective on what it means to be healthy in each of the realms I mentioned and then offer a few words on the resulting wholesomeness that arises from this healthy consistency.

Mental health - To be mentally healthy means to be generally inquisitive and curious to learn every day, to reason from first principles (such as the non-aggression principle), and to actively pursue any available means of unleashing the full potential of one's own intelligence.

Emotional health - To be emotionally healthy means to have devised an inner world of boundaries and permissions that allows one to reflect upon and integrate the origins of one's own emotional states while maintaining a trend of increasing personal contributions to the glory of civilization and the assurance of humanity. Maybe read that one again.

Spiritual or philosophical health - To be spiritually or philosophically healthy means to live in accordance with natural law, whether you perceive it to be set forth by God or by spontaneous order. Moral trespasses against this natural law weaken your constitution. Serving natural law strengthens your constitution.

Physical health - To be physically healthy, from my point of view, is to have a diet and exercise regime that directly supports your ability to fully manifest your intellectual, emotional, and moral capacities. Eat too much of what makes you feel sluggish? Cut it out! Remain immobile to the point where you cannot sustain massive effort as a culture warrior? Step it up! Movement unlocks physical health.

Artistic health - To be artistically healthy is to constantly refine and hone an aesthetic that serves virtue, love according to philosophical principles, and the advancement of human civilization. Artistic unhealthiness would be to adopt an aesthetic that is cynical, ugly, grandiose, or self-absorbed and thus apart from human progress.

Social health - To be socially healthy is to succeed at the social roles attributed to your biological sex. Generally speaking, men protect, fight, lead, divine, and discern. Women nurture, organize, nest, and soothe. Those who utilize these roles to create communities, tribes, and societies for the raising of children are the most socially healthy. We look to philosophers, business leaders, politicians, and religious institutions for leadership and insight on how best to attain this social well-being.

You begin to embody wholesomeness as you piece together these areas of health. We can spot wholesome people by the way they radiate positive influence out into the world. They are beacons of humanity that set right to wrong. They remind us of our innocence and help us to taste the sweetness of life. For example, Donald Trump reminded us of the sweetness of life in a potential world of true justice by encouraging chants of, "Lock her up!" against Hillary Clinton. We build on these successes to foster more wholesomeness in the people around us. Put the sword to your cynicism and join the wholesome in re-envisioning a better world.

Being reliable (Opposite: being a flake) –

So far we have covered encouragement and wholesomeness as being vital tools for rising in the hierarchy. The last one I will cover is the quality of being reliable. To be reliable is to be a person who consistently accepts more and more responsibility in

life, with respect to philosophically advancing the
species, and delivers on those responsibilities.

Every single interpersonal connection or
opportunity for connection matters. When we can build
up the discipline of being reliable, we become good
shepherds of the truth. We begin to amass a flock or a
following. We are steady through the storms and we
deliver our people to themselves. None of this can be
accomplished if we are punch drunk from our battered
histories and only infrequently in the mood to do right.

Have you ever met someone who was "on" all the
time? They can be relied upon to vigorously engage in
the efforts necessary to "get the job done". There's a
consistency to their whole manner of being that allows
us to trust them. They respond to our emails *if* we offer
value that will help them to advance their virtuous
mission in the world. They speak to the world on a
consistent schedule. They show up to events where good
people congregate. They decry every abuse that comes
their way. They keep their appointments. They do not
show up drunk, moody, petulant, or evasive. They are
sturdy and robust.

We need reliable people in the culture war. Can
you be relied upon? What goods can you deliver, on
time every time? What value you can you offer to those
higher, abreast, and below in the culture war? When can

we expect your contributions and for how long? The longer, the better. The greater the contributions, the better. Keep it timely, keep it consistent. Put in work!

There you have it, a brief primer on rising in the hierarchy. You may only rise in the hierarchy of good and merit if you have skills to offer. Encouragement, wholesomeness, and reliability are vital skills but remember that greater things could and will likely be asked of you by people higher in the hierarchy. This book is a primer on getting into the culture war as a culture warrior. More nuanced and sophisticated skills will be required by the generals of this war. They deal in spy craft, intelligence, power broking, strategic silence, and other things probably above my "pay grade". Consider me a sergeant and this is basic training. Off you go!

The Quality of Fatherliness

In a society of high divorce rates[4], the importance of quality fathers cannot be overstated. The quality of fatherhood is inexorably linked to the health of cultures. Due to the expansion of the welfare state over the last 40 years, the West has seen fathers replaced by government programs. What has resulted has been a distinct lack of quality fathering for the Generation X and Millennial generations. We see that these generations have tended toward the Left in their political affiliations[5]. With fewer fathers around, Gen X'ers and Millennials in particular, have too often developed into entitled, whimpering, and apathetic citizens with little sense of social cohesion or engagement.

We need these generations to develop a "psychological backbone" and rediscover, en masse, the qualities of fatherliness. Without a firm resolve to reinstitute fatherhood in the family unit, the West will be overrun by more dedicated competing societies. We need young men, now more than ever, to look long and hard in the mirror and give up their reluctant tendencies. In doing so, these men will not only yield to the West happier and healthier communities, they will save her from the onslaught of political Islam.

---

[4]https://www.washingtonpost.com/news/wonk/wp/2015/06/23/144-years-of-marriage-and-divorce-in-the-united-states-in-one-chart/
[5]https://heri.ucla.edu/PDFs/40TrendsManuscript.pdf

Fatherliness is a personal quality comprised of several characteristics, the foremost being *protectiveness*. Through a philosophical lens, protectiveness is the ability to distinguish in-group from out-group and to defend the in-group from an out-group. The primary in-group is the nuclear family unit itself, but considerations of nationhood, culture, political ideology, and religion can also be made. A man can build up his ability to serve as a protector to his family in any of the following ways:

-owning guns; practicing gun safety and target accuracy

-maintaining physical fitness such that a violent attack from an out-group assailant could be met with lethal force if necessary

-practicing situational awareness in all environments where the man's family will be

-owning a trained guard dog or a guard dog breed

-choosing a safe neighborhood for one's family to live in

-exercising good taste and psychological judiciousness in terms of the people and information a man allows into his home

Another characteristic of fatherliness is *assertiveness*. Assertiveness is the ability to bring to bear one's preferences on a given situation. Assertiveness serves good fathers in that it allows the father to take a leadership role in the family, community, and society. Fathers must act as shepherds for their children. A father does so by making it abundantly clear to all out-group members that the needs of his family will be the underlying consideration in his dealings. A father without assertiveness is a father who infects his children with passivity and docility, making them vulnerable to predators, dangerous guides, false mentors, and corrupt authorities.

The last characteristic of fatherliness discussed in this essay will be the role of *providing* for one's family. A father who provides for his children is a father who is willing to go out and brave market conditions in order to add value. Without his provision, children will look to the mother for this role. Mothers are not natural providers. A provider must be willing to sublimate his aggression into pro-social, ethical strategies that put food on the table and a roof over his children's heads. A father's self-efficacy is tied to his ability to provide for his children. A father may build up his ability to serve as a provider to his family in any of the following ways:

-take paying work in the market economy

-learn salesmanship and customer service

-research employment trends and initiate a career in a promising field

-climb the corporate ladder

-strike out into an entrepreneurial endeavor

-learn marketing, persuasion, and branding

-go through an apprenticeship leading to gainful employment

-practice people skills

-go to a post-baccalaureate program that is in the hard sciences and correlated with in-demand positions

-save every possible dollar to put toward compounding interest arrangements

-take an active interest in family men who have been successful at providing for their own children

Attaining the quality of fatherliness requires the current fertile generations to make an important change. Western civilization needs young men to regain their sense of candor for children and their ability to be strong adults in the face of the globalist deluge. Fatherliness must again be a prized pillar of our culture. Otherwise, our civilization will fade away.

Choosing Your In-Group

Identity is the sameness across individuals. It has to do with personality, history, genetics, psychology, culture, and spirituality. You have some choice in who your in-group is. The most efficient way to do this is to discover your identity. When you find it, you can easily choose people who share some of your identity and get along with them. The more you share an identity, the better you will get along, most often. Identity isn't the be all, end all. It does provide a useful launching pad into social connection, however.

It is important to note that identity is relatively fixed whereas you can practice a lot more choice in terms of who you associate with. You can choose to identify as a woman. Yet cutting off your penis to leave an open wound you constantly have to reopen and clean does not mean you are now a woman. It just means you are a psychotic self-harmer and everyone should be relieved you took yourself out of the gene pool.

Another one: you can identify as Will Smith (God help us). You can dance around in hip hop videos, kiss your grown son on the lips, hang out with oil-rich

Arab princes, and hate conservative white Americans, but the choice to do these things does not make you Will Smith. One does not simply declare, "I am Will Smith" and suddenly embody his identity.

Identity is maybe 80% pre-determined and 20% up to choice, roughly speaking.

Take the author, for example. I am a straight, white male. Cue the cascade of screeching urban liberals to drown me out. I was born to a mother from an influential, upper middle class, Castizo, Roman Catholic conservative family. Most of the men were engineers, ranchers, or clergy.

My father's staunchly middle class, conservative, Roman Catholic family emigrated to America in the middle 1800's and he is equal parts German, northwestern European, and Scandinavian. The men from his side were dairy farmers and ranchers. My paternal grandfather served in WWII and was decorated for his service.

My mother's temperament is fairly open, highly conscientious, somewhat extraverted, highly agreeable, and slightly neurotic. My father's temperament is slightly open, highly conscientious, slightly introverted, somewhat agreeable, and somewhat neurotic.

There is no history of diagnosed mental disorders in my family. No criminals, drunks, or sexual abusers. There is slightly more poverty and lower IQ on my mother's side. There's no poverty on my father's side and my father's IQ was tested to be in the 130's. His father was highly intelligent as well. There has been high academic and middle entrepreneurial achievement on both sides of my family.

From this information on my life you can surmise the following:

-I am mostly European

-I tend toward agrarian, outdoorsy sensibilities

-I am conservative

-I will not slip into poverty, drunkenness, or criminality

-I am somewhat open, highly conscientious, split on introversion and extraversion, fairly agreeable, and slightly to somewhat neurotic personality

-I am highly intelligent but not genius level

-Roman Catholic or familiar with Catholicism

-high academic and middle entrepreneurial achievement

You, too, can work up a similar survey of the basic facts of your existence. Be sure to include the big five personality traits[6] since they're all the rage these days with people who suspect personality is transmitted genetically. Once you have a survey of who you are at these basic levels, you get to find people who are like you.

Here's who I will gravitate toward:

-people who seek high intellectual achievement

-white people who have a similar cultural background

-people who appreciate agriculture, animal husbandry, systems thinking, and spiritual types

-mild affinity for soldiers but little to no direct involvement with them

-Catholics, former Catholics

-agreeable people with slight neuroticism

-law abiding, sober, non-criminals

Birds of a feather will flock together. Much of this is already decided when you're born. Some people get outlier genes and end up with some sort of

---

[6]Extroversion. Agreeableness. Conscientiousness. Neuroticism. Openness to experience.

dysfunction present in their extended family. For the most part, we're a product of our two family trees.

Choosing an in-group comes naturally to most people. It is the Establishment that slips lies into people's heads via schooling, media, and academia. Whites[7], the focus of most cultural and racial vitriol in the modern era, are told all sorts of nasty lies about who they are:

-they're work-resistant welfare addict school shooters who can't dance

-they're inherently racist and therefore owe welfare to non-whites

-they should breed out their race for the good of everyone else

-they are generally liberal and vote for bigger government

-they hate the environment and trample it underfoot

-they are dumb, inbred, corny, and perverted

These are all projections or outright lies invented by globalist propagandists. The only real inherent weakness of whites is their pathological

---

[7]Blacks are a close second, due to Democrats treating them like pets for generations.

altruism, their tendency toward universalizing morality for out-groups who do not reciprocate. This, however, is a massive weakness. It has led to the downfall of the West. I digress.

Choosing your in-group involves the decision to say, "This is who I am and I will support people who are like me." This doesn't mean you give up all autonomy, become an evil collectivist, and engage in online race war as some milquetoast intellectuals would have you believe. It simply means you accept yourself as you are, appreciate and seek to honor who you came from, and become an advocate for who you can be in this world. It doesn't mean you chuck out values, such as free speech, and choose people solely on identity terms.

If a consanguineous, congenitally disabled, Arab homosexual with low IQ, high neuroticism, and a history of criminality wants to devote himself to helping people who are like him, I am not going to stand in the way. Neither will I be very likely allow him into my hypothetical homeowner's association made up mostly of white, straight, Christian, low criminality, low neuroticism ethnic European peoples. He can have his fiefdom in the Middle East and I will help my people out over here in the United States.

It is in my higher IQ, mostly ethnic European genetic interests to see more people like me in this world. Together we bring into existence the kind of society that I find ideal. Except for a few strains of mankind[8] that seem to be genetically preloaded with self-loathing, most people feel this same way about the people they're genetically aligned with. This is natural. This is healthy. No need to fight against this with some kind of misguided sentimentalism masquerading as an argument. Our in-group boils down to who we each are. For the most part, I have no interest in sharing an in-group with a congenitally disabled Arab homosexual. Certainly I have no genetic interest in helping bring about his worldview into existence. Neither does he have any genetic incentive toward my worldview, so long as I'm not forced to give him welfare. And who knows, maybe we can find some middle ground on shared values...

It's okay to be distinct and be explicit about it. There's no harm in it. In fact, most of the harm comes when governments decide to mix us up and inflict us with draconian anti-speech laws.

Obviously you don't want to choose the people who are in your personal life simply and solely for the fact that they share genetic and cultural similarities. But odds are that the people who end up being in your personal life will share these traits. In your personal life

---

[8]including white liberals

you get to practice voluntary association (voluntarism). Who you choose to associate with will often be dictated by your life goals, conscious or unconscious, and your personal values:

-Some people think highly of themselves and have the competence to deliver on that belief, so they choose moral, virtuous, healthy people to be around.

-Some people think highly of themselves but do not have the competence to deliver on that belief. They choose vain, incompetent, insecure, but perhaps sometimes moral and decent people.

-Some people think poorly of themselves and have the competence to deliver on that belief. These people will cause problems in society, relative to their level of intelligence, and will choose immoral, unethical, and unhealthy people to be around.

-Some people think poorly of themselves and do not have the competence to deliver on that belief. These people will take what they can get. Often they go on welfare or go to countries with lower standards of living.

To summarize, people tend to band together based on:

-intelligence

-ethnicity

-religion

-culture

-language

More choice is practiced in the following areas:

-profession

-politics

-living situation

The most choice is practiced in our personal lives according to:

-self-image

-level of personal virtue

-psychological health

There are so many ways that people group together, but nature has a specific set of characteristics for us to come together on. If all you got from this essay was some mild resentment that I used the phrase "congenitally disabled Arab homosexual" at one point, this book is sure to challenge your worldview!

How Tribes Work

The social structures and institutions of the Internet are ahead of those in the physical world. On the Internet we are seeing influence centered around great thinkers and tinkering businessmen, not central governments and banks.

As such, we could, within a generation or two, see society reshape itself around great thinkers and tinkering businessmen in the corporeal world. We might see the soldier class, which has long enforced the predations of governments and central bankers, switch its loyalty to those people with large platforms on the Internet. Were this to be the case, society would take on a much more feudalistic and free market quality as opposed to the current globalist paradigm.

With society centering itself around thinkers and businessmen, we will see identity shift away from consumerism and multiculturalism into tribalism and nationalism. Society is becoming accustomed to unending access to information, transparency, and open free speech. One can congregate with others who share their values and identity like never before. There will only be more of the same as time goes on, come what may with the longstanding statist institutions of the world and their fiscal debts.

Slowly but surely, people are coming to understand they have a lot of flexibility in terms of where they live, who they associate with, what currencies they trade in, and how they express themselves. Central banks and their precious corporations are losing their position as trendsetters. The globalists are losing their grip on the culture.

True freedom of association will eventually make a return at a legal level. Once this happens, the floodgates will be totally open for people to cluster as they wish. The smartest will cluster around thinkers and tinkering businessmen. Those thinkers and businessmen who have the strongest tribes will be the ones with the most influence. They will form voting blocks. They may form autonomous societies with borders and barriers to entry, provided alternative, decentralized technological and defense system platforms emerge.

Given these potential outcomes, it is a good use of one's time to begin now on the question of forming a tribe.

The first step in building a tribe or joining a tribe is to step out of social isolation. Take to social media or some other public sphere of influence to voice your opinion and share your learning process. You will begin to draw people to you who share your values and identity. You will also repel those who don't like who you are or what you stand for. Bonds of trust and strategies for influence will begin to emerge for you as you continue to learn. Your ideas and ability to convey your ideas will be tested.

You can find a tribe by understanding the concepts of hierarchy, as outlined by this book, and through a self-knowledge process. Self-knowledge will yield to you an understanding of your identity, your ability to add value in a hierarchy, your weak spots and tendencies to drain energy from others, how to hold boundaries with your weak spots, and how to figure out your existential purpose in life.

An accurate sense of hierarchy allows you to accurately identify the leader of a tribe, who is close to the leader and for what reasons, how entry into the tribe is gained, and what out-groups the tribe is in competition with. Knowledge of the leader of a tribe allows you to study the influence, power, and persuasion dynamics at play in the tribe and how they are effectively wielded. Understanding who is close to the leader offers you an aspirational path to gaining more influence in the tribe. Those close to the tribal leader often make for useful mentors. Entry to the tribe is important because it involves entrants swearing a kind of allegiance to the standards and customs held by the tribe. You need to know what personal sacrifices you will have to make in order to be accepted.

Knowledge of the out-groups competing with the tribe matters because at some point the tribe is going to come into conflict. Clarity on the tactics and strategies of out-groups readies you and your tribe for their advances, feints, and defensive postures. We will cover the tactics of globalists in the essay on Saul Alinsky's *Rules For Radicals*. Every tribe needs its members to understand how to navigate the conflicts it will engage in if the tribe is to last for any duration.

In relation to a tribe, which is a group of people centered around an identity and purpose, a person will need to know who shares their identity. Identity is comprised of a person's highest philosophical values, and their genetic and cultural heritage. The degree of similarity in identity will generally determine the degree of automatic empathy between parties. Automatic empathy is a psycho-evolutionary advantage in the struggle for influence, power, and persuasion between tribes. The clearer a person is on his or her own identity, the more readily they will assimilate in with similar people.

Sometimes, particularly in the more philosophically consistent tribes, we will need to mobilize our own individual creative capacities in service of the tribe. Economics are the bottom line of any social institution and we *will* be required to contribute money to the tribe.

Weak spots and one's own personal narcissism or grandiosity will harm the cohesion of a tribe to the degree to which the leader or leaders are healthy themselves. A young member who desperately reaches out to those far above his rank in the hierarchy to try and be seen for his worth will undermine the operations of the tribe and reduce his own prestige. When you are early in the ranks, you show your merit rather than speak of it. It is not the place of one low in rank to offer meta commentary on the operations of the tribe nor to impose his own ego upon those above him.

The tribe serves those at the top, foremost. Those high in rank hold the prized leadership skills and abilities that all others must pay a toll to access. A person must commit themselves to these leaders or be shunned and ostracized. This imagery is as much true in medieval times of feudalism as it is in the current, psychological times of the Internet.

There will always be cranks and nihilists dwelling in intellectual hidey holes. They will hope to drag in any grandiose, misguided youth who have left the security of conventional society. It is as important to steer young people away from globalism as it is to steer them away from nihilism. The cranks and nihilists love picking off stragglers.

The most noble of tribes are the tribes that uphold justice, reason, empiricism, and humility through philosophical first principles.

With self-knowledge a person is able to gain the empathy needed to make an educated guess at the motives of the leaders of the various tribes. A person is then able to choose for themselves what tribe they will belong to. Some people will stand with the philosophers on the hill. Some will choose the bribery and corruption of globalist overlords. And then there's the stragglers that get picked off.

Tribes propagate the most foundational principles or assumptions of their leaders. Do we choose the most noble? Do we choose the most capable? Do we choose the most terrible? Do we choose the most powerful? It is a personal, speculative investment each of us will have to make.

Building Up A Conventional Life

Most everybody wants to run from their demons by trying to project some grand vision of who they are. Far fewer want to be true to themselves by facing their own demons. In our modern day society it is simply easier to focus on "who to be", drink some coffee, and let most other concerns fade into the background. The problem is that no matter how successful one becomes at "being someone", people's unresolved stuff eventually becomes transmitted to the next generation.

Self-knowledge involves finding out where your "operating system" is working on flawed assumptions. This means reflecting upon your emotional experiences in a deliberate and structured manner. Doing this isn't as sexy as simply sublimating the emotional pain into some societally approved pose. "My dying mom who neglected me liked it when I made her laugh while she was in the hospital bed. I guess I'll be a standup comedian!" is an example of this. Another would be the Muhammad Ali, "Some kid stole my bike. I'm going to beat the hell out of him and any other mean looking kid who crosses my path…for decades." Sublimating emotional pain simply puts you on a life track that will never leave you fully satisfied with your existence. You may become wealthy, famous, or powerful but you'll never feel fully resolved.

The path of self-reflection offers the chance to build your entire life upon solid foundation. By doing this, you break the intergenerational cycle of abuse and stop living in ways that alienate you from yourself. With the intergenerational cycle of abuse broken, future generations will no longer have to deal with the burden of "who to become". Instead, these generations can use self-knowledge to live in the world.

Healing from childhood trauma is not a sexy, glamorous life choice. Most, but not all, of the massively lucrative work in the world involves some level of dissociation and self-deception. Taking lots of selfies, punch other men in a boxing ring, make people laugh and then go home and hate yourself, so on and so forth. The good news is that the world is changing. Just the other day a psychotherapist made headlines in a major news publication for her claim that, "working mothers are producing mentally ill children and that the problem is at an 'epidemic level.'"[9] The more society comes to prize philosophy and self-knowledge, the easier it will be to make more money and still have a truthful relationship to yourself.

---

[9]http://www.dailymail.co.uk/femail/article-5451309/Psychotherapist-warns-working-mothers-produce-mentally-ill-children.html#ixzz59lKhHh14

People who choose the self-knowledge path often come in with grandiosity and say things like, "I'll be just like Warren Buffet and have all the success he's had." They become paralyzed by the prospect of matching his mountain range of work and level of genetically inherited intelligence. In such a grandiose state, people are unwilling to take a sober account of their own histories, their capacity to work themselves to the bone, the trajectory their parents' parenting efforts put them on, and to what degree they possess natural-born intelligence. It's all or nothing. Become Warren Buffet or be a paralyzed loser who has no output. This is a crippling mindset to be caught in. Thankfully, there is another way to approach greatness: you build up from the basics.

We have the choice to build up a life of conventional success. I call this a "conventional life". We don't need to dismiss the conventional world of business as "soul-sucking corporatism" or "working for The Man." Instead we can view more conventional means of obtaining a paycheck as grounds for practicing what could become a high flying career as a content creator or philosopher down the line. For example, being a purchasing agent at Walmart Corporate Headquarters in Bentonville involves the following skills and more:

-negotiating shipment sizes

-checking over quality assurance

-tracking shipments

-coordinating with inventory and sales reps

-coordinating with research

A person who isn't a stuffed up Marxist can look at this kind of work experience and find a way to synthesize it into a higher skill set, based in the free market and helping to drive philosophical discourse forward.

Striving to have a strong résumé or CV, adding value to a conventional business, and gaining industry-specific skills need not be viewed as a jaded black hole of "normal". These aspects of our life can inform our work, particularly when we don't come from a background as well-parented as a Pewdiepie or as philosophical and brainy as a Stefan Molyneux.

Grandiosity can be summed up as the inability to match expectations to personal abilities. It can also be termed an "excess of self-esteem". Many young people, in their grandiosity, make choices that put off the important, steady work of living an adult life while tending to one's own needs. They get face tattoos, STD's in third world resort towns, or dress up like Nazis. Such people are incapable of reality testing and need honest feedback from others. Grandiose people are often unable to see the merits of earning a conventional paycheck while building up their professional and people skills. Their path will eventually lead to nihilism. It is crucial to give grandiose people non-pathologizing, assertive feedback so that they can begin to course correct.

The freedom movement could benefit from having young people willing to do the boring, small reps that actual greatness is built upon. Over time, such people become fully formed adults who won't burn out because they have an actual personality core to lean back on when times get tough. This is the path that builds the best fighters. The "be somebody!" path is a premature launch that cripples the most enthusiastic.

A steady paycheck, regular hours, and a hierarchical business structure is the best social program there is. Most of the men who have had the biggest impact on philosophical progress in the world come from this kind of background. Steady work builds steady constitutions. A working man's attitude toward doing something truly worthwhile in this world is a winner's attitude.

Assertiveness & Forthrightness

In your personal dealings it is important to be assertive and forthright. Together these qualities give you presence and help you to be more memorable to others. When you are memorable to others, it is easier for them to connect and reconnect with how they take an interest in you. The more you are remembered, the more influence you have. Some men, mostly unconsciously, want to be remembered as villains and traitors. Some want to be remembered as noble philosophers or arbiters of justice. Then there's everyone in-between.

"Assertive", according to Merriam Webster, is defined as, "disposed to or characterized by bold or confident statements and behavior". Let's hone in on the "confident" component of that definition. Confidence is the result of competence. You gain competence by mastering skills associated with the discipline. Confidence is the knowledge that you have a certain level of competence. When you are competent at an endeavor, you will speak with assertiveness to those with less skill than you. You will know what is necessary and appropriate given the conditions of the moment and bring into awareness that knowledge. Those who have more skill than you at the endeavor will be assertive more so with you than you will be with them.

Some men use assertiveness to be bold and break into levels of mastery they wouldn't otherwise attain. They rise to the occasion. The boldness component of assertiveness is important because we need to constantly innovate, learn, and grow in order to remain connected to our sense of purpose in life. Assertiveness allows a person to break new ground.

A master in a field of endeavor will choose to be bold and assertive with reality itself. He may reach rarified air, where he has few contemporaries. In such cases, the master is working with the metaphysics and deep programming of society. Oftentimes this man must "go it alone" as there is no one left to guide him in his decisions. He has grasped the highest complexities of a chosen endeavor.

Those at lesser levels of competence will practice less assertiveness against reality itself, but there is no greater teacher, is there? We all can learn from testing ourselves against reality. We need those greater than ourselves to assert to us when we are not testing against reality but against some fragment of our histories. We climb the ladder of skill and awareness by speaking with more experienced parties.

"Forthrightness" is defined as "directly forward, without hesitation". This is a quality best practiced with consideration to reciprocity. Does the other person in this relationship practice forthrightness to a similar, lesser, or greater degree than myself? To be forthright with a person who does not reciprocate the value can be folly. Sometimes we need to be forthright and accept the consequences, especially in the court of public opinion.

The next essay in this book, "Ask and Earn", will help elucidate forthrightness as a means of allowing us to attract those with similar goals and repel those who would undermine us. We establish our position and observe how others respond. With assertiveness and forthrightness we do not chase others. We plant our flag in the ground and see how things shake out.

In dealing with the public it is important to understand that there is a baseline level of bigotry and intelligence to contend with. The average IQ in the USA is a catastrophically low 98[10]. Combine this fact with public schooling being responsible for turning people into socialists and it may not be favorable to be fully and totally forthright. President Donald Trump's favorite book is *The Art of War*, a book that deals in the art of deception and assertion as a means of winning military struggles. The principles outlined in that book

---

[10]https://iq-research.info/en/average-iq-by-country

are incredibly informative when it comes to knowing how to surf the bigotry of public opinion. Reveal too much truth and people's discomfort will cause them to simply tune you out. Reveal too little truth and people will lose their faith in you or worse, mark you as a bad actor. There is an elusive, shifting median point at which truth can be spoken to the world. *Rise and Fight* and *The Art of War* in combination will help you to discover for yourself how close to the mark you can strike. Another extremely useful book is Scott Adams' *Win Bigly*.

Assertiveness has to do with presence and confidence. Forthrightness has more to do with vulnerability, admission, and efficiency in communication, given conditions of reciprocity. Together these qualities give us a picture of person who confidently presents himself but can be plainspoken in his purpose, without trickery or wordplay. For some personalities, plain-spokenness is good persuasion. We can imagine a Midwestern type fellow who shakes hands, kisses babies, and can be seen atop a tractor wearing overalls. In other cases, plain-spokenness can come off as too naïve and too dumb. Knowing when to use intrigue and when to bring transparency is a skill that the practice of assertiveness and forthrightness in your *personal* life can inform.

At the outset of your work as a culture warrior, assertiveness and forthrightness are best practiced in the home and among loved ones. As you learn these basic skills or dispositions, the weight of your experiences will help you to understand how you will deal with those belonging to out-groups. Some foes and competitors are agreeable and can be confided in. Some will require you to guard closely your true opinions.

Ask and Earn

Most people have a general sense of what they want. They want personal fulfillment, earnings, a healthy and happy family life, to belong to something, and personal freedom. Most people give up on having these values in their life to the fullest extent possible. Their ability to deliver on their ambitions and aspirations falls short. They settle for less. They stop believing in themselves. They internalize voices of discouragement, apathy, and fear.

This isn't necessary!

We need to give ourselves the best possible chance, given our degree of emotional maturity and intellectual capacity, to attain the values we seek. We do this by asking others for help.

When we ask for what we want, we signal to others that we are in pursuit. How could anyone possibly know what we want in this life unless we tell them? The more people that know what we want, the better positioned we are to succeed. This is the basis of marketing. Billboards are a way of saying to a passersby, "We want you to buy this." If businesses and corporations get to signal to others all the time what they want, why shouldn't we as well? If our efforts are noble, let's try to reach as many people as possible!

Of course, you could go the route of zero self-knowledge and wildly proclaim to society, "I want cocaine and hookers!". You may even get what you want, but it will never be as satisfying as getting what you need. *Wants* are so often tied to assuaging discomfort. Instagram is filled with physically beautiful people advertising and obtaining their wants in life. *Needs*, on the other hand, are tied to the resolution of trauma and our capacity for contributing to society proactively. To find out our needs we need to self-reflect. Generally we will find that our needs fall along the lines of personal fulfillment, earnings, a healthy and happy family life, to belong to something, and personal freedom.

Personal fulfillment, what many term the "spiritual life" or religious devotion, is associated with existential questions such as:

-What is my purpose in life?

-How do I serve the needs of others to the best of my abilities?

-How can I learn to love myself?

-How must I accept myself as I am?

-How do I redeem myself from my rotten childhood and live as a hero in my own life?

-How do I humble myself before the truth or God?

Questions of personal fulfillment are the bedrock of self-knowledge and involve the core assumptions we have about ourselves. When we ask society for help in our pursuit of personal fulfillment, we seek out people who are wiser than ourselves. We ask around. We behave in a forthright manner. We let it be known to those we trust that we're sorting out the fundamental assumptions we have about ourselves and could use some pointers. "Who's the wisest person you know?" we may ask a friend. We delve into questions of philosophy and seek audiences with philosophers. We may go into therapy or find a mentor. We may pray to God.

Earning a living in this world involves understanding, through trial and error in the marketplace, where our skills and talents are most-valued. One can only *earn* a living through ethical business practices. Generally speaking, one does not "earn" a living working in government unless that position effects a reduction in government spending greater than the amount of one's own salary. Most people want to earn their way through life, knowing that the work they have done was ethical. In no small part due to public schooling, most people are misled on how to do that.

When we go about figuring out how to earn a living, we let it be known that we want to earn our keep. We look at who is hiring, reflect on how we can add value to their enterprise, and send in our credentials as a means of asking to join in the work. We ask friends and family if they know of opportunities. When we are in an organization, we ask strategic questions of our superiors in order to learn the responsibilities they hold. We ask around for the choicest trainings available for our industry. We take to the Internet and research the skills that would take us to the next level. Without decent, paying work, we are unable to take part in the culture war. It takes money to put thrust behind ideas. Content creators and platformers need a war chest to take down the mainstream media. The further we integrate ourselves into the economy, the more opportunities we can offer to others looking to fight for civilization.

A healthy and happy family life is vital for the propagation of society and the species. This is the primary pursuit of most heterosexual adults. When we ask society for help in this endeavor, we place advertisements of ourselves on dating websites just like a local business placing an ad in the classifieds. We build up our bodies to signal to others that we are made of prime reproductive material. We ask our friends, supervisors, philosophers, mentors, and family to help us out by keeping an eye for potential mates. We may take a public stance on an issue in the hopes it will net us the kind of dating success that could lead to a family.

When we have a marriage partner and are in the process of building up a family, we ask for help by looking to other families for insights into their successes and failures. Their support in this most important of civilizational endeavors can make all the difference. Our children get to have other adults and children around. This benefits the health of the family.

To belong to something involves understanding one's own place in the human social hierarchy. Self-reflection in this area of life could include questions such as:

-At what level can I realistically affect change in society?

-Who is above me in the social hierarchy and why? How do I gain their confidence?

-Who is below me in social hierarchy and how can I be of service to them?

-What experiences from my history could be keeping me from rising?

-Am I facing any health, relationship, or financial issues that are preventing me from rising?

-What has been my historical trajectory, as determined by my parents and their parents, in the social hierarchy and how can I go to the next level?

Once a person has a sober, empirical understanding of their own social standing, they may reach out to society and ask for help in an accurate manner. This is most effectively done by starting a business and then garnering client and customer feedback on the efficacy of the business in delivering services. This is an explicit process involving social media feedback, data analytics, sales figures, and surveys. Sometimes it is an empathetic process wherein the business owner simply gauges the emotional state of the client or customer. Asking does not mean "begging" or being a doormat when you're turned down.

Entrepreneurship, at a fundamental level, is the process of a person voicing their own aspirations and ambitions for society. As the economy turns more toward a permission-based economy, fewer and fewer people will be able to get what they *want* and will instead need to focus on what they *need*. The entrepreneurship of the future is here. Empathy is more and more a part of meeting the customer's needs. This type of business acumen will become the gold standard if the globalist banking elites are stopped from enacting their plan to flood the West with low level IQ economic migrants.

One final component of "Ask and Earn" involves forming community. Community is formed around shared values. From the point of view of this book, self-knowledge is the highest value. Desperately few communities have been formed around this value. With this book and others like it we will see conditions improve.

We gain community by searching for or hosting events and gatherings with like-minded folks. We invite others to join in our company. We go through measured courtship process and watch as our purpose for being together deepens. We identify with each other more and more. Hierarchies form and our community works to see our values advanced in the world.

When we ask of the world we must be willing to provide equal value in return. Reciprocity requires a humble persistence to consistently learn and grow. Those who reciprocate judiciously will be well rewarded. It requires discipline to maintain healthy reciprocity over years and years. Nobody goes very far based on self-absorption alone.

Politics Attracts The Best and The Worst

Politics is a highly contentious field because it is the field that deals with government power. Government is the institution of violence. He who wields government has a monopoly on the violence wielded in the land. Government puts limits and restrictions on the way we live our lives. Government is comprised of governors, those who govern.

Politics and government attract the absolute worst power seekers and occasionally a reluctant hero.

Nowhere else but government can a person ascend to such legendary fame or descend to villainy and infamy.

It has been scientifically proven that having power over others is a recipe for corruption and addiction[11]. The more power you acquire, the greater the chance you will stamp underfoot innocent people. This is the nature of power, it requires ever-increasing responsibility. In a just society, people take power reluctantly and act as conscientious stewards of an institution that could fly out of their control at a moment's notice. In an unjust society, people take power jealously and sell their nation's sovereignty to the highest bidder, through warfare or welfare. Either way, there's no one to oversee government. There's no third party watchdog that can actually dissuade government's course. This is why politics becomes the perfect place to act out.

To "act out" means to replicate the harmful, negative experiences one had in their psychological development. Here are some examples to illustrate the point:

-People who were sold out by their parents over some inanimate object will sell out their country over some uranium to Russia[12].

---

[11]http://www.dailymail.co.uk/news/article-2136547/Power-really-does-corrupt-scientists-claim-addictive-cocaine.html

-People who had their souls murdered will send young men and women off to die in foreign lands needlessly[13].

-People who were sexually abused will use their influence to try and sexually abuse others[14].

Round and round the cycle of abuse continues in an unjust society. Socialism settles like a shroud over the land and unspeakable horrors begin to crawl out of the basements where they have been kept. Politicians have power over the innocent and they let all of the skeletons out of their closets. Rumors start to spread that ritual sacrifices of children are being made. "Satanism" becomes a conspiracy theory that mounts evidence and credibility as time goes by.

The question to ask those who are drawn into politics is, "Are you repeating your history?" It is almost as if the entire mainstream media machine is designed to avoid forays into this line of questioning and keep out anyone who would be able to formulate this question. If people were to connect the dots that sickos in government are originally created in childhood, there

---

[12]http://www.breitbart.com/clinton-cash-movie/
[13]http://dailycaller.com/2015/08/31/donald-trump-wanted-last-republican-president-impeached-for-foreign-policy-lies/
[14]https://www.nytimes.com/2017/07/18/us/dennis-hastert-released.html

would be a social revolution. Maybe we'd see some high level child molesters hang in public trials...

The old saying goes, "Washington is Hollywood for ugly people." There is no limit to the narcissistic supply a person can gain by steeping themselves in politics. Hillary Clinton is the best contemporary example. She got to be a star for thirty years by riding the political coattails of her husband and by selling her soul to the highest bidder. Politics offers a chance for a person to try and validate all the quiet lies they've told themselves about themselves over the years. Hillary got to be the heroine in her own story, constantly drugging herself with power in order to not feel the emptiness her wretched parents infected her with. She'd die of a heart attack if she had to feel all that pent up rage at once. Bits of it seem to make her go on drinking benders and take tumbles down steps.

However rare, there are genuinely decent people working in government and seeking political power. Most of these people are from the Founding Stock of our nation and they work quietly to little acclaim. There are some who gain media access and use it to spread the message of liberty and the will of the silent majority. Senator Rand Paul and Kansas Secretary of State Kris Kobach are two standouts. Some great men from history to consider are Senator Charles Lindbergh,

General George S. Patton, Thomas Jefferson, Richard Nixon, and Calvin Coolidge.

Donald Trump will have two terms to work with as President, unless he fails to build a wall along the southern border. He will have eight years to prune the government apparatus of redundants, traitors, and incompetents. If he is a great President, he will make it much harder for career criminals, charlatans, snake oil salesmen, and sycophants to succeed by turning to the state. If he is an average President, America is so loaded down with losers and criminals that the government will collapse under its own weight into Brazilian style socialism. If he is a terrible President, we can probably count on being micro chipped and having our children taken to transexuality camps.

Donald Trump's history tells us that he has the potential to be the all-time greatest President if he is able to overcome his flaws.

It is important to keep in sight a person's background prior to engaging in politics. What is their track record? Did they overcome personal difficulties by helping others to be morally successful? Are they convicted criminals, divorcees, or deadbeat parents? Were they raised by such people? Are there scandalous pictures of them on the Internet? We need this information so that we can understand what potential strengths and weaknesses they will display once in office.

At this point in history, it's the Left versus the Right. Globalists versus the West. The West is deeply divided between everyone who would like to sell the West's sovereignty out to corporate and banking interests and the those who have the interests of the nation at heart: the Trumpian/nationalist right wing and European nationalists. It's important to understand a candidate's history in order to predict how they will perform in office, but it's just as important to remember that the Left has given up all pretenses and is madly clasping at power. There is no middle ground anymore.

The Left is the political movement that uses crime as firewood to light the funeral pyre of the West. The Left lacks people of conscience, self-reflection, and collaboration. The nationalist Right has all the great men of history. This is the score. This is how it has always been, only the clarity of the dilemma is right at the surface. There is no more pretending. There are no more shades of grey. We are witnessing the final showdown between those who act on their unconscious histories for evil and those who have some wherewithal to better themselves and others according to rational standards.

Who To Take Advice From

No talking head on the Internet is free of the consequences for the behavior in their personal lives.

This observation came to mind for me recently when I was watching four or five prominent right wing platformers waxing eloquently about how gender relations ought to be. Each of them were so sure of themselves, so confident. I know for a fact that none of them are married. Only one of them is in a committed relationship. None of them have committed themselves to raising their children peacefully, if and when they have children.

Round and round in dazzling circles they spoke to each other as an audience of one thousand people listened in. Only one of them, and coincidentally the one I respect the most, referred to the earned wisdom of a person with some actual qualifications to speak on gender relations: Jordan Peterson. This person was quickly told that women shouldn't be telling men what to do under any circumstances. The rest of the panelists and the audience were delighted at a woman being "put in her place". I watched this woman quiet herself and submit to the psychological abuse traded as currency in this discussion on gender relations. Nothing of any substance was said for the rest of the panel but boy, there was a lot of fighting and Internet blood-sporting!

If we peer past the clever tweets, the polished talking points, and the prodigious output, we get to determine whether or not the person in question has the lived experiences to inform their opinion. Some people call this "authenticity". Can a person who claims to know how women and men ought to relate stand by their claims if they've led a life of miserable romantic failures? Can a person who has never empathized with their own experiences as a child really speak to us about how children are best raised and educated? I say "not so much". Of course, a messed up person can make a great argument now and then, but are they in a position to give interpersonal advice? No.

Some panel conversations can go round and round and never hit any salient, actionable points because the panelists lack basic self-knowledge. Some well-meaning panelists let a clearly toxic person into their midst. The toxic person cajoles and pesters them for 90 minutes and no real, personal or political progress is made for anyone participating. The audience got to see a verbal battle, sure, but the toxic person got attention and a bump in their numbers. This is how the

Right has long operated. Meanwhile, Democrats are flooding across the borders and infiltrating the institutions.

Not all panel discussions are like this. These kind of discussions comprise maybe a quarter of the total panel discussions taking place. Their content is better than television, granted, but much of it is the back and forth fencing of people's unresolved emotional issues masquerading as intellectualism. Overall, I see these conversations as necessary and useful, particularly to those who have little background in the "course material", but neither are these conversations the end-all, be-all. They have inherent limits. Meanwhile, the enemy operates behind the scenes, frequenting their donor parties and Democratic Socialists of America meetings. The enemy is doing actual political work.

Panel discussions, in general, can give us interesting intellectual ammo, clever wrinkles on historical events, and ideas on how the world should be run. They do not point out to us means for personal transformation at an existential level. That is not the format and it would probably be boring if someone tried to make it that way. Panel conversations are populated by people who track the news cycle and rely on the books they have read.

These people are often fighters and advancing freedom in the world. But are they self-reflective? Will they "go the distance" in their personal lives over the decades to come? I certainly hope so. I hope this message reaches some of them. The price for ignorance of your inner experiences is steep. People who fail to take their inner experiences seriously are destined to repeat themselves for years and years. At some level their personalities flatten out and they remain emotional children, even those who made it to biological parenthood. They are content to infight, choose lesser opponents out of personal insecurity, and meta-politic while the world burns.

Truly, there are substantive and informative YouTube channels everywhere out there. I donate money to a number of them. Everyone is doing necessary work at whatever level they are conscious of and intellectually capable of. These are all encouraging developments and I would not raise a finger to stop someone from watching the content of even the most glib and safe right wingers. Everyone has different intellectual needs and the market will decide what is popular.

The lack of self-knowledge I am pointing out often triggers feelings of humiliation in others, so I do not do it in a direct way, naming names and telling people in the moment how little they know themselves. That would be cruel, arrogant, and counterproductive. I keep this message confined to this book, where people pay money to be provoked and challenged. This way it is better understood and less confrontational.

Who enjoys being told their intellectualizing can be a distraction on account of their personal issues with addictions and dysfunction in their personal lives? In panel type discussions it's a kind of "harshing the vibe" thing to do and boy, does it stir up the denial of the audience tuning in for the intellectual swordplay. People experience this as "psychologizing" and usually they are right to feel defensive since most people who do psychology are leftist dickheads.

Lack of self-knowledge is a vulnerability, in the negative sense of the word, of many prominent right wingers. The Marxist deconstructionists, particularly the highly empathic and psychologically trained ones, are well aware of this. They know how to turn the personal, self-knowledge deficits of nationalists into opportunities for derailment, infighting, drama, unproductive "side quest" discussions, and all sorts of other obfuscations.

Right wing platformers will exhibit symptoms of their own lack of self-knowledge in these primary ways:

-infighting and "patrolling" members of their in-group

-withdrawal from conflict and a loss of productivity

-spiritual compromise in order to gain relief from clashing with the establishment

-doubling down into unearned, false certainty so as to avoid moments of genuine vulnerability and reflection

-loud proclamations of "loyalty" to a larger platformer

These behaviors are visible every day from people in the nationalist in-group. Now and then a person is open to some support. Admitting vulnerabilities in the middle of an information war can lead to disastrous consequences and the very least, lost time. We are all marching through this time of tremendous uncertainty. This puts stress and hardship on us all. However, we don't have to be victims of the age we're in. We get to be proactive. Having people around who remind us of our nobler selves can make all the difference.

Soldiers prayed before and during battle. Self-knowledge can be a prayer, a dialogue with the best and worst sides of us. Prayer, of the Christian order, is making a big comeback. This kind of reflection can help us to find our way and do what needs to be done.

Overcoming Friendlessness

America is facing a loneliness epidemic[15]. Due to mass migration, loss of civic engagement[16], the rise of secularism, and the expansion of government, Americans are shutting themselves up in their dwellings and seeing social bonds fade into nothingness. Loneliness itself has considerable health implications, particularly in old age. Loneliness increases stress hormones and inflammation while also increasing a person's risk for dementia and Alzheimer's[17].

Facing loneliness at an individual level is a challenging task because of the bevy of distractions

---

[15]https://www.nytimes.com/2016/09/06/health/lonliness-aging-health-effects.html?action=click&contentCollection=Well&module=RelatedCoverage&region=Marginalia&pgtype=article
[16]http://a.co/i4E3USL
[17]https://www.nytimes.com/2017/12/11/well/mind/how-loneliness-affects-our-health.html

available to us. There are computer and phone screens to gaze into while social media platforms collect surveillance data on us. Air flights are cheaper than they have ever been. Mass migration puts an unconscious dread of procreation in the minds of most young people, owing to the strong correlation between racial diversity and ethnic conflict. Cats and dogs are now bred in absolute abundance across the country, offering people a mild substitute for human relationships. So on and so forth the distractions go.

It is a basic human need to be vulnerable, to reveal oneself emotionally in the presence of others. Whole systems of tribal dance, ritual, and song were once employed toward this end. As a result of this loneliness and social isolation rampant across America, young people have fewer friends than ever.

Friendlessness resulting from unaddressed loneliness is a social problem affecting countless well-meaning men across the USA. Male achievement has been driven underground by feminism, multi-culturalism, and the welfare state. Men born in the mid-1980s and after have inherited a society where they no longer hold a cultural hegemony. It's no longer preferable and cool to be a straight white male. The last predominantly white male culture that held institutional status was grunge music in the early

1990's. Since then, America has seen a rapid decline in cultural standards toward ghettoization and multicultural sensitivity.

In order to rise to cultural prominence as cultural arbiters, straight white males will have to overcome the problem of friendlessness. To do this, they will have to learn the value of friendship. Friendship begets tribes. Tribes beget influence. Influence is power. Power is useful in recovering the major institutions: banking and finance, schools, industry, cinema, music, sales and service, tourism, and government.

This essay will focus on the actionable, immediate, and personal steps a person can take to find friendship.

The basic foundation of friendship is enjoyment in the company of the other person. In order to be an enjoyable person to be around, a person will have to learn to become competent at charisma, honesty, boundaries, structure, loyalty, and consistency.

Charisma is a magnetic charm or appeal. Here are some worthwhile personas to study in order to gain charisma:

-*John Wayne* - grit, ruggedness, handsome, protected the in-group against Indians, distinct vocal quality, unstoppable force for justice in his films, fatherliness, utilized his height, anti-Communist, anti-PC

-*Winston Churchill* - supremely grave, erudite, massive vocabulary, killed the out-group, charming drunk, master of verbal jousting, round like a melon and dressed like a gangster, made a mother figure out of every woman who came into his orbit

-*young Brad Pitt* - the ultimate seducer, haunted, handsome as a glowing Norse god, wounded lone wolf, irreverent and elusive

-*Robert Redford* - also handsome like a Norse god, the human equivalent of a golden retriever, elusive yet reliable, excellent use of a reluctant smile

-*Napoleon* - master of artillery, hard-charging, lovestruck, calculating, short temper but never a scoundrel about it

-*Ernest Hemmingway* - morose, plainspoken, big time fan of baseball, womanizer, drunk, open shirt and hairy chest, lover of the outdoors

-*Don Quixote* - pursued his dreams to the ends of the Earth, easily misled, ferocious temper, escape artist

    The list could go on and on. Charisma can be learned. One useful YouTube channel for this study is Charisma On Command[18]. Study those who have massive social influence and discover in them qualities that you possess yourself. Build up those qualities as an artist would, through conscious and deliberate practice.

Can you defy your enemies with the "knowing smile" antagonism that Donald Trump is able to? Can you look a woman in the eyes even 25% as much as George Clooney has been able to base his whole career off of? Can you wear your shortcomings on your sleeve like Robin Williams was able to? Can you tell a story with one tenth the gravitas that Orson Welles was able to? Mimic these people and soon you will gain some measure of their abilities.

You have the ability to shape your persona, the manner in which you present yourself to others, according to the full capacity of your abilities. Go to an improv class, try stand up at an open mic, speak to a mirror or a YouTube audience, go to Toastmasters, perform music, and put yourself in other situations where you engage your personality through presentational means. Doing this will give you the practice you need. Mimic the greats. Learn their tricks. Employ them at your behest.

Honesty serves friendship because it gives both parties an accurate gauge of everyone's preferences and

---

[18]https://www.youtube.com/user/charismaoncommand/videos

desires. Honesty helps us honor each other's' preferences and provide each other encouragement when it comes to attaining our desires in this life. Honesty allows us to be vulnerable in a way that doesn't manipulate the other party. We get to work out conflicts and get going in the right direction.

Structure allows us room to breathe in a friendship. Getting along on the Internet, which involves little actual interpersonal contact even with Skype, is a far cry from spending time with another person in-person. 4chan, Twitter, and Reddit simply train us to trade quips...or paragraphs at the higher end of discourse. It's awkward to spend time with someone you've only known online until you start to build an in-person rapport. Here are some ideas:

-meeting for coffee and then going for a walk

-starting out as workout buddies

-any sport under the sun (basketball, tennis, cycling, golf, racquetball, etc.) where the friends have a similar skill level

-meeting up at a conference based on shared values

-go to a political rally

-hiking

-rodeos

-orchestras

-county fairs

-billiards and beer

-jamming on instruments

Participating in an activity together allows people to get a sense for one another. Video-gaming together does not count. Put a time limit on your hangouts and watch as you become more comfortable over time. You come to understand how a person regards rules, boundaries, competition, social norms associated with the structure, and their own level of emotional mastery. You get insights into their presence and body language.

Loyalty is the recognition of personal in-group association in the face of social uncertainty. Want to keep your friends? Don't sell them out to anyone at any point. Don't laugh at their expense ever. Don't toy with their trust. Choose them over people you don't know, every time. Show them support if they come under fire. Do them favors if they have favors stored up with you. Measure their worth against the out-group, not ideal standards of perfection. When they confide in you, keep their trust.

Consistency is key for friendships. You simply cannot maintain friendships if you flake out or quit. Flakes and quitters are poorly regarded by healthy society. Nobody likes a weakling or a quitter. If you say you are going to do something, do it! Don't puss out. Show up. This allows people to trust you and begin to count on you. Trust over time yields intimacy. Friends who are consistent with each other even just lifting weights form a much stronger bond than friends who meet on a scattershot basis and hope something comes out of it.

It's worth repeating that for overcoming friendlessness in this politically correct society *you have to meet in person*. It does not matter if you live several states away from each other. Save up your money, buy a plane ticket, and spend a long weekend together. Make sure the effort to meet is reciprocal and the bill is evenly footed. If it goes well, you may want to negotiate living nearer to one another. It is not easy but it is necessary if you want a friendship.

You have a choice. Handle your friendlessness. Friends are not the end all be all. Passing on your genes and being a provider is more important. That being said, if you can get all your ducks in a row, you are going to be better off because friends help.

The Trauma Ward

"Some guys they just give up living
And start dying little by little, piece by piece
Some guys come home from work and wash up
And go racing in the street"

-Racing In The Street, Bruce Springsteen

A lack of emotional sustenance in childhood
leads to disillusionment with civilization in adulthood.
If a boy or a young man wasn't taught about the
sweetness in life, how could he possibly understand
later in life what is worth fighting for? We have
generations of males to rehabilitate. As a society, the
West still has little understanding of the basic failure of
fathers to sons and the aftereffects.

The fathers who fought in WWII were
emotionally cauterized by the agony of killing their
European brethren en masse. In turn, they built a
society of comfort and correctness with their machinery
of industry to help them cope with the loss. The Boomer
males were the Television Generation. They trudged to
work as pawns for a global banking and media elite
from 1968 to 2014, when they started to die off in
significant numbers. Easy credit, globalization, and the

fear of being labeled a "racist" cajoled them into turning their children over to daycare centers, video games, and the meat grinder of politically-correct public schooling.

Now our young men are "soy-boys" and "bugmen". They freely sexualize one another and laugh at the madness their deconstructive heckling has wrought. They hate. They hate it all. They cloak themselves in this vitriol. They cast contempt at the few upstanding among their generation. Back and forth they rock, waiting for their feeding tube of entertainment and sex to come down from the ceiling. They will vote to destroy. They will cast themselves at the feet of foreign hordes of starving rapists seeking iPhones and sneakers.

The world wars never ended. The military industrial complex simply took it to where it could not be easily observed: the psyche. The drugged imps inhabiting our cities are but fragments of the full human beings that launched themselves into the meat grinders of 1917.

In a few of these soy-boys and bugmen there exist dormant embers: faint, distant whispers of tenuous hope. Your empathy will help you locate the tiny distress signals embedded in their personalities. Boundaries are the precision tool that will peel away the rot. Encouragement will feed the flames.

With respect to these kinsmen who have lost their way, are in a trauma ward. We must work diligently to revive and sustain those who can be saved. The soy boy or bugman you can save may be your coworker or your brother or your neighbor. He is in your sphere of influence. Practice your influence and work diligently. Ply your resuscitation skills at the level you can and then move on to the next case as quickly as possible.

Here are some practical considerations to make, working within the trauma ward metaphor:

Empathy –

Find the pulse. Greet the weakened man on the hospital bed with your curiosity. Do not beleaguer him with your judgments and admonitions. He's not yet conscious enough for that. He's clinging at the edge of life. Ask him questions. Find out what matters to him. What gives him hope? Why is he still living? This is the pulse.

Boundaries –

Don't take the bait when death beckons. The bugman disease infesting the patient will attempt to pull the conversation downward. The patient will deflect. Stay on course. Do not fight but do not yield. Remain assertive and hold fast. Make it known that degeneracy, sarcasm, nihilism, and vanity will not be fed here today. If the patient needs to air out the toxicity he's bottled up, let him. Remain calm and centered. Eventually the survivor in him will start to show. Stay centered on the pulse, his will to live.

Encouragement –

When his being is ready for it, give him a blood transfusion. Use your personal presence, your empathy, and your sense of goodness in the world to speak to him in a way that will strengthen his pulse. Give him the truth, but do not make the soup too rich. He is weak. Give him what he can handle and move on to the next man. Come back around again when he has processed the infusions of courage. Give him his space and respect his autonomy. You are not raising up dependents.

When a man has recovered sufficiently, he will begin to walk on his own two feet. He will get around more and more. He will begin helping the others in the trauma ward. Eventually he will be able to leave and go back to the battle. He will return not as a bewildered boy abandoned as armies move in to clash but as a man capable of commanding his circumstances. He will remember the kindness shown to him in the trauma ward by the doctors, nurses, and orderlies. He will return from time to time to offer his encouragement. He will know the process of personal redemption and be capable of regenerating himself whilst in the thick of battle.

You have a reason to use your empathy: to restore your countrymen. You cannot save anyone who is resigned to death, but walk about the trauma ward calmly speaking the truth and you will see who stirs. Go to them. They need you.

Bugman Repellent

"In this hollow valley
This broken jaw of our lost kingdoms"
-T.S. Eliot

From UrbanDictionary.com, a "bugman" is defined as:

A bugman is your typical big left leaning city dweller. He is usually obsessed with consumerism, lining up to purchase the newest iPhone or MacBook when it comes out, and using a smart watch/smart home speaker for longer than the week after he bought it. Chances are he owns other throwaway smart gadgets as well. All his tastes in movies, music, expensive food, art, and more are determined by what review sites and blogs say.

Everything about his personality and life is not defined by who he is, but by what he buys and his consumerist tendencies. He'll be subscribed to at least one, maybe multiple subscription services, he'll happily use social media and upload all of his information to the cloud, and he'll gravitate towards things that seem "rational" and use big words.

Yet there is something big missing about his life, something that can be seen in his face. Something that can be seen the minute you strip away all the consumerist choices and realize, there's nothing else. His life is empty, hollow, and all about serving corporations, until he dies, and this is seen in his empty, insectoid stare that implies he's dead inside, giving him the name "bugman".

These are our modern day "hollow men". They have been hollowed out by the lack of true, masculine sustenance in their families and in their societies. In some men all that is left is the bugman and they are condemned to nihilistic death and non-entry into the gene pool. We need not bother with this type. Dead men walking.

The second type of bugman is the one who quietly holds aside some part of him that knows there's more to his life than vapid, leftist nihilism. You will know him when he steps *toward* you as you speak the truth. He may come baying and cackling, but if he comes at all he can be turned toward himself and away from death.

Not all men can afford a constant orderly to help them regain their lost potential. Some of these men laying on the beds in the trauma ward need magazines to peruse, so to speak. Let's start with the cultural features, the types of "magazines", that are likely to be to contributing to his current, debilitated state:

Cosmopolitanism –

We should not offer the bugman more "city living" in ever dwindling spaces. City living has softened him and disconnected him from the natural rhythms of nature. Western man no longer looks to the stars because they simply aren't visible anymore. He resides alongside peoples more suited and accustomed to the crammed, polluted environment the city offers. Work and coffee, rinse and repeat. The coming of the garbage truck and the domestic disputes of his alien neighbors mark his sense of time. Cars rush by on the nearby highway, ever present. Police sirens are everywhere. If his city is "enriched" enough, there are Muslims driving vans into crowds of people. The pigeons defecate on his stoop, mixing their toxicity with the leaves of another year gone by in the hum of the city's armpit.

This is not to say that all city living should be avoided. In a culturally homogenous and capitalistic society, a middle class intelligentsia springs up in the cities. This type of white collar work is tremendously important in articulating the direction a society will go if freedom is to be maintained. This essay is articulating the kind of cosmopolitanism that sets in once the heart of a city is lost to globalism.

Consumerism –

The bugman in his afflicted state must be disconnected from his gadgets. No more gadgets! No more gadget vendors telling him what electronics to adorn his rented bedroom with. He is something more than this. The gadgets distract him from his inner life. He has no idea who he is. He needs be alone with his thoughts. He needs to feel his feelings. He needs to reflect on who he has been and who he could become. He needs the constant whack-a-mole of his gadget addled consciousness to slow down.

Scientism –

The bugman worships government and government science. He thrives on the easy comfort of memorized factoids. He believes he can oppose entire arguments with factoids. Always with the factoids! He cannot perceive the queer, milquetoast nature of his government funded celebrities. "God is dead!" they say to him through his gadgetry. Science cannot convey meaning, only particles and statistics.

Pornography –

The bugman is anesthetized from his body. His diet of microwavables give his brain bursts of browsing time until the caffeine wears off late at night. Then he surrenders himself to the low intelligence, San Fernando Valley whores who practice debauchery with strangers. His hand and his member die a little death with the help of the bottle of lotion kept nearby. He agonizes one more time as the witchcraft on the screen fades out of mind. This is the only stimulated portion of his body, likely circumcised, and only for 5 minutes of the day. Perhaps it happens several times a day. Death smells his ejaculate and comes like a vampire bat to feed in the night. His dreams are of post-apocalyptic wastelands and video games. Slowly he becomes more deviant and self-suspicious.

Now for the "magazines", the cultural features within this metaphor, we can leave at his bedside table. What follows is an outline of a culture of true masculinity that the bugman can steep himself in. These themes are imbued with courage and philosophy, crucial nutrients he needs to turn back the years of insectoid avoidance of life.

Pastoralism –

The bugman will need to be reminded that he comes from pastoral stock. His kind was once Western, not digital-Asian. America was made great by men who knew the rhythm of nature, the needs of animals, and the significance of the seasons. The bugman needs to be presented with images of natural splendor and men atop the mountains. He needs to wonder at the stars in the sky. He needs to remember the hunters in the wood and the farmers in the field. Perhaps he needs to see tremendous homes of hearth and home industry at the edge of settled society. He needs to go for a frickin' hike in the woods!

Craftsmanship –

The bugman consumes and consumes like a fetid cockroach. He will need to learn how to create rather than consume. His hands must be put to work in the service of creation instead of masturbation. He can grip tools rather than thumb the screens of his gadgets. We can show bugmen how to do the "jobs that only the Mexicans do" as immigration dries up. The glory of gaining mastery over the corporeal universe must be conveyed to him. Could he build a home? Even a tiny one?

Philosophy –

The bugman needs somewhere to place his love of logic and consistency. We can show him the great philosophical struggle being carried out by great minds across the West. We can demonstrate how those who adhere to principles are able to influence the decisions and perspectives of those around them. We can show him how his Big Brain Atheist heroes are miserable bugmen themselves without a connection to some purpose greater than their own.

Family –

Pornography is a cult of male surrender to silicone witches and globalist-voting pimps. To break this paradigm, the bugman must understand what responsibilities and dispositions are associated with the upkeep of a loving, productive home environment. He must be shown the stories of people who are bound together by love, not by greed and sexual perversion. He must come to understand what a delight children are. Our stories must illustrate the cooperative sensibility between man and woman, the gravitas of their wholesome connection and partnership. We must place him, psychologically, in situations where he cannot reveal his member and stimulate it.

There are many more antidotes to "bugmanism". This is a good start. We must remind the bugman of his true, mammalian nature. He is not a composition of gears to process video games and Mountain Dew. He is of flesh and blood, made to build, love, and defend.

Perspectives: Mark Collett
twitter.com/MarkACollett
thefallofwesternman.com

Mark Collett is the author of *The Fall of Western Man*, a book chronicling the many aspects of the West's degrade. He runs a popular YouTube channel debunking the myths propagated by the UK's media establishment.

-How has Western man fallen and how does he regain his standing?

The healthy and natural social structures that shaped generation after generation of Western man have been weakened and removed in order to prevent Western society from holding on to its culture and traditions. This has destroyed strong and cohesive Western communities and reduced them to disparate groups of individuals who are only concerned with hedonistic and selfish pursuits.

Whilst Western societies have broken down, huge numbers of immigrants have entered the West and retained their culture and ways of life and now pose an existential threat to those of European descent. In order for Western man to rise again and defend himself and the lands of his forefathers he must reject poisonous ideologies such as feminism, Marxism, materialism and hedonism and embrace what made the West great: tradition, culture and of course, the foundation of any strong and healthy society – the nuclear family!

-What are the traits every man should aspire to in order to wage the culture war most effectively?

Men must be strong – in all senses of the word. Men must serve as pillars of the community, as husbands, fathers and as an inspiration to the next generation and as such, every man must reach for excellence. Men should strive to be intelligent, moral and physically fit. It has always been men that have risen to the challenge when it came to defending Europe and to do so men have always had to come together, to facilitate this coming together we must rebuild cohesive communities. In harsh times people gather around beacons of hope, in order to save Europe, men must rise up, be willing to make sacrifices, be brave and courageous and willing to stand up and be counted – as such these men will be like beacons of hope around which strong communities will form.

-Why is the West worth fighting for?

Western civilisation represents the greatest achievement the world has ever known. Those of European descent led the way not only in science, technology and engineering but also in art, literature and music. But all the magnificent achievements that are spread across the Western world did not come about by accident, they all sprung forth from those of European descent. To see those people vanish, to see them be bred out of existence, would see the end of a bloodline that is responsible for not only the greatest technological marvels the world has ever known, but also the most inspiring art and literature ever produced. The West is worth fighting for because those of European descent are priceless, they are irreplaceable, they rose up from the edge of ice sheets and whilst others looked to the stars, those of European descent reached out and touched them. Europe's magnificent flame should never be allowed to falter for if it does the whole world will be a darker and colder place.

Patience, Persistence

"Rome wasn't built in a day." -French proverb

Some people have the "it" factor. They can draw attention themselves by way of an overpowering, magnetic charisma that renders those in their vicinity utterly charmed and delighted or in shock and awe. Sometimes it's through dazzling good looks. Others have a prancing wit and unending verbosity. Some people know how to get a crowd moving. A background in the performing arts lends a heavy hand to the success of these people.

Perhaps you feel you can't simply gallivant your way through life like these high flyers. Intense focus and attention to the things you do, particularly in front of higher IQ audiences, will allow you to do some of the spectacular things mentioned in the first paragraph of this essay.

When you are building your platform in the culture war, you must proceed with patience and persistence. Some of the risks you take will pay off. Some will fall on deaf ears. If you are not a particularly charismatic person, a lot of what you do will fall on deaf ears. That's okay.

Personal charisma takes time and focused effort to build, especially if you've had a rough background. Building up the ability to create meaningful, useful content and somehow combine it with your hard-won charisma can be, and usually *has* to be, a long-spanning effort.

People who are great at twenty, and there are more and more of them out there, started as young as eight. They likely had parents who nurtured their talents and helped them to hone their skills.

If you feel you have to struggle to get another five subscribers or followers, it's simply where you are at. You can't magically sprout epic boobs or a rapist's wit. You can't upload 2,000 books into your brain or stumble your way into becoming independently wealthy.

You are simply going to have to take your licks and stick with it.

Persistence is the long game. A lot of people can pick up a few hundred followers or subscribers by putting out average efforts that tease at something greater. The choice to keep at it even in times of stagnation will distinguish you from the rest of the pack, even if it is to a limited audience. This shows your audience that you care; You are a dependable, reliable person who will put the shoulder to the wheel to push and push. This is where the hard-won charisma starts to come in. You start to move out of being perpetually lazy or unlikeable, perhaps even pathetic. You work the muscle of success and eventually you'll be more and more rewarded.

The frustrating Catch 22 with becoming a healthier and healthier person in a fairly unhealthy society is that you become less and less relatable to more and more people. This is why, aside from giving life-encompassing effort (the "so good you can't be ignored" approach), everyone can benefit from considering using a shtick, a persona, in order to break through to the masses:

-Maybe you are known as the high school aged black guy who cleverly breaks down leftism while wearing full suits to class.

-Maybe you have pretty eyes, are of mixed origin so leftists can't play the "racist" card on you, and you ask easy questions, allowing for a wide swath of people to come on your show.

-Maybe you fill the Sage archetype nicely and make long, flowery videos on the meaning of psychology and the value of life.

-Maybe you are kind of a dunce and willing to make an ass out of yourself so that people are disarmed when they listen to you go over conservative talking points.

-Maybe you are a razor sharp intellectual who is prone to few mistakes and you have a penchant for talking to anyone about almost anything.

The point is that patience and persistence make all things possible. Your persona, your shtick, will come out in time and some people just don't need it. What matters most is the hard, persistent work. Not everyone is an overnight success. Maybe you don't come into the full strength of your potential as a culture warrior until your 40's or 50's. That's okay. Do right by others and by your civilization, year after year, and the good effects will accrue to your being.

Go get em'.

Tradlife

The deck is stacked against families. Big Money in America[19] is doing everything it can to get women into the workplace and out of the home where they are the happiest and most productive. Every college and major corporation offers special incentives to bring women into the workplace. Young women across the

---

[19]and the CIA

country are fed a disgusting diet of vapid music[20] and Hollywood perverts[21] meant to debase and deflower them. Women are told they are equal to men and thus deserve equal pay. Little girls are routinely sexually molested, sold into sex slavery[22], and exposed to migrants from third world rape cultures[23].

Now, more than ever, we need to be encouraging women toward attitudes, habits, dispositions, methodologies, and relationships that serve to bolster Western Civilization, not undermine it.

Fortunately, there is some good news. Divorce rates are dropping[24]. There are a host of young women who are championing traditional family values online such as Wife With A Purpose, Lady Lily, Brittany Pettibone, and Faith Goldy. Donald Trump is in office and while he's had a rocky history of divorce, two of his sons have large families with obvious conservative values in place[25]. Hollywood is hitting historic lows in

---

[20]https://www.billboard.com/charts/hot-100

[21]https://www.vanityfair.com/style/2017/10/jennifer-lawrence-shares-story-of-sexual-assault-at-elle-women-in-hollywood

[22]https://www.csmonitor.com/USA/2016/1018/FBI-sting-shows-child-sex-trafficking-still-thriving-in-United-States

[23]http://www.breitbart.com/big-government/2016/08/10/twin-falls-refugee-rape-special-report-refugees/

[24]http://time.com/4575495/divorce-rate-nearly-40-year-low/

[25]One of his sons has recently divorced. And so it goes, eh?

revenue[26]. Family values seems to be the new counterculture.

Perspectives: Wife With A Purpose

gab.ai/Wifewithapurpose

wifewithapurpose.com

-What is tradlife and why does it matter?

Tradlife is short for "traditional life" and it means the restoration and preservation of traditional values. We live in a time, post the 1960s, where every value and every tradition we have as humans and as a civilization have been either challenged, reordered or stripped away entirely.

It is important that we identify and restore many, if not all, of our traditional values and practices as a people. These values are time-tested mechanisms that our ancestors developed through blood, sweat, and tears for forming and maintaining a functional, healthy, civilization. Without them our civilization will literally cease to exist.

-In a nutshell, what is feminism and what has it done to the West?

Feminism is the idea that a woman who serves her loving husband and children is inferior to a woman who serves a boss who hates her. It's the idea that men should have no

---

[26]http://www.breitbart.com/big-hollywood/2017/09/02/worst-box-office-in-25-years-hollywoods-problems-are-permanent-deep/

rights in family court systems. It's the idea that women should be chosen first and foremost in every venue of life despite the fact that women-led societies, the world over, have never developed past the stage of eating berries and living in mud huts.

Feminists will tell you that feminism is simply about the equality of the sexes but they forget two important things. First, equality does not exist. No two people on earth are equal. Men and women are not equal in interests, passions, pursuits, desires or ability.

Second, they forget that the cultural ideal is not the cultural reality. They may sincerely want some form of equality yet they ignore the fact that while they chase after this notion of equality, the reality they create is one where women have become harsh, mean and unhappy.

Furthermore, they create a reality where men are constantly being told they are inferior: from the time they are little boys at school and girls wear shirts saying "Boys are dumb, throw rocks at them" to the times when they are in college and if they are drunk and a girl is drunk, they are accused of raping her even though they were both, equally, inebriated.

When men start a family they live under the constant threat that at any moment, for any reason, their wife can leave them, accuse them of any horrible crime she can think of, take his children away from him forever, take half of what he has built in his entire life, and then half of what he makes *thereafter. Men know this, women know this, and hence men must cower to the domination of their wives at all times and in all places or risk losing everything.*

-What do women and children need from men in this day and age?

Women need men to take power again. The biological reality is that women have no power over men that men, as a collective, don't voluntarily give us. Men have an instinct to make women happy, and normally that's a good thing, but as we have stripped the social norms and conventions -our Tradlife values- from our civilization, women's worst nature - that of constant demands and unruliness- has been allowed to run wild and fester without the natural checks and balances from a healthy male population watching over us and protecting us. Protecting and providing for women often means protecting us women from our own shortcomings too. I know that puts a lot on men, but that's just the natural balance and reality of life.

We women and children need loving men to tell us "no." Judges to say "no, ex-wife, you can't claim your husband abused you with no evidence and get sole custody of this man's children." Male doctors and law makers to say, "No, women, you may not murder that man's child simply because you are the one carrying it in your womb." We need father's to say, "No, daughter, you may not listen to that music or go out with those bad friends, I love you too much to let you ruin your life." We need husband's to say, "No, wife, I love you but our children need their mommy to be home with them while they are young. I want you to focus on creating a lovely space and childhood for them where they feel you are devoted to them, not a career."

Tradlife has less to do with the girliness and pretty hairstyles that some platformers would have you believe and more to do with what Ayla, Wife With A Purpose, has delineated here. Tradlife is not an opportunity to pass off the laziness post-modernist society has infected you with onto your husband in an effort to disappear from view. It is a familial choice to *undo* female vanity, male temerity, and step into a future that serves civilization. Without good women to lead other women by example, such a movement would not pick up steam in the public sphere.

The Madness of Modernity

This is where the book gets ugly for a few pages but these things must be said. Modernity is the quality of cultural and societal dysfunction resulting from the rejection of reason in the West, starting around the French Revolution. If we want to be nitpicky, we could term this phenomena "post modernity" but, for the sake of brevity, let's stick with "modernity". Some of the major characteristics of modernity consists of city living around central banks, the rising tide of third worlders piercing into the West, psychology as the replacement of philosophy, radical egalitarianism, toxic altruism, lifestyle over identity, the deconstruction of the family, and the flattening of social hierarchies. Through philosophy we are able to pierce the haze of modernity that has settled over the land like a toxic blanket. This essay will be demonstrating the madness of modernity as well as positing a new way for man, centered on reality and philosophy. Some of this essay will echo points made in "Bugman Repellent".

Reason

With the advent of common law and reason in the Middle Ages as the means of resolving disputes, Western man was finally able to begin to break out of the cycle of corruption and madness. Centuries of relative progress and prosperity were halted when Western man began to instead follow "philosophers" and playwrights who were all about the "feels" instead of the "real's". This resulted in the French Revolution, Franco-Prussian War, WWI, and WWII. These massive bloodlettings severely weakened the West, killing off the hardiest and most courageous of the European stock.

Since the final, massive European fratricide of WWII, the West has been struggling and failing to reclaim her former glory. Simply put, there is a tremendous absence of the kind of men who struggled to make the West glorious in the first place. Imagine a world where there are multiples of your heroes, working in conjunction. A basketball team of five LeBron James'. A rock band with two Freddy Mercury's. A White House with Donald Trump Jr. and his more handsome twin, Thelonious Trump. You begin to get the picture.

Instead, as Mark Collett mentioned earlier, the West is now seeing an invasion from the intellectually bereft third world. This migration is an attempt by the globalist elite at filling a tax base shortage but the scheme results in lower quality work and societal discord. All of this is aided by the Western welfare state. The migrants who have come to Western shores in the past three or four generations are extremely jealous of losing their newfound existence in Western society to the natives who object to their presence. Underscoring all this, we have a pensioner class maintaining a death grip on all the major social institutions.

The few good men who remain in the West are making considerable efforts at awakening the rest of society from the ills of modernism, the nihilism of having lost generations of the best men, and are pointing out the subpar standards third worlders are burdening the host societies with. The work has been slow-going but notably aided by the proliferation of social media. In order to retake the mantle of glory and be worthy once again, Western man must re-embrace in-group strategies and self-knowledge. These tools are his edge against the unfeeling submission of Islam and the rabid technocracy of Asia. With self-knowledge and well developed in-group strategies, Western man will be able to live in reality, grieve the loss of so many glorious brothers in the World Wars, and hold strong boundaries once again with the third worlders who feel entitled to the fruits of his labors.

City Living and Central Banks

The economy is run by a billionaire elite consisting of globalists and the descendants of what are often referred to as "old money". This elite, having been known to participate in weird mystical rituals, runs the economy through central banks.

The central banks are privately owned, not beholden to the public. They manage the currencies of nation states through expansion or contraction of the money supply and setting of interest rates for lending. These manipulations of the economy are done to personally enrich the elite. The rest of us poor bastards live or die by their whims. Billions and billions of dollars routinely vanish from government budgets and into thin air. Now journalists are starting to disappear into thin air[27].

The greatest heroes of recent times so often have been the brave men who oppose this power structure and take steps to implement alternative systems. Usually they are assassinated by agents of the bankers[28]. No measures have yet proven successful in imprisoning and bringing to justice the members of this secretive power cabal.

City living relates to the madness of modernity in that the distribution of reserve currencies into the economy happens through government borrowing money from these private bankers and spending the money into the economy through government programs. As such, there are massive distortions in the economy that emanate from government power centers. People intuitively understand that to be near a major center of government is to improve one's chances of becoming wealthy. Thus we see the true power and influence of places such as Los Angeles, Washington D.C., London, New York City, and every other major government center in the world with central banking.

---

[27]https://www.louderwithcrowder.com/tommy-robinson-arrested-jailed-for-recording-muslim-gang-rape-trial/

[28]CIA and US State Department

Western man saw the rise of mega cities only in the past hundred years. As such, he is not acclimated to the conditions brought on by central banking and big government. These conditions are akin to captivity for Western man. He develops what are termed "neuroses" and he is tended to by the globalist dark science of psychiatry. With brain altering chemicals he is able to continue on in massive density urban cityscapes, pursuing the centrally printed greenbacks that allow him more stuff, more coffee, and perhaps a feminist wife or casual sex at a nightclub.

Western man, through the immigration policies put into place by the hyper elite and their minions, is suddenly taken from the Alps and the hedgerow fields of gold and placed into direct competition against coolies from afar. These foreign-imported coolies are able to outcompete the formerly tall-standing and farmyard bred whites because they have lived in conditions of squalor, urban density, and rabbit level breeding selection since time immemorial. These are, of course, generalizations meant to get to the heart of the matter. We all have known a few noble, high intelligence migrants[29] to the West, but they are exceptions to the rule.

---

[29]https://en.wikipedia.org/wiki/Shiva_Ayyadurai

It is well understood that grass fed, free range beef results in the highest nutrient content. Western man has yet to figure out, en masse, that the same applies to humans. Tiny apartments in mega cities are the same as tiny pens for pigs in massive slaughterhouses. Still, Western man is in a state of hypnosis and drawn to the hum of the government printing presses like moths to a flame.

It is the work of philosophers to alert Western man that he has placed himself on the conveyor belt to oblivion. He must be inoculated against the numbing doses of "feels" (out-group empathy) that are injected into him as wearily he glances around to see foreign peoples flopped beside him, rutting in their beastly welfare greed. Soul death and cancer await him so long as he is spellbound.

Western man must sober up, leave the cities or fortify himself within them, arm himself, and wait as these cancerous tumors burn out. His alternative is grim. He will be swept up in the killing fields as the socialist, welfare-borne zombies of the third world are unleashed.

Rising Tide of Third Worlders

Western man, by allowing himself to be co-opted time and time again into wars that only served a globalist banking elite, left himself mortally vulnerable. He fell into a stupor of nihilism, watching as the treasonous poison of Marxism destroyed the notions of a nation state and the family. He became infected with toxic altruism, all too readily handed down to him as a narcotic by the administrative state. He sent his fortune overseas, feeding or killing the vacant mouths of foreigners. He adopted starved, primitive children who saw a temporary IQ bump as their conditions improved until they, as adults, regressed back to the mean and quietly resented their host nation. He gave "power" to women and welfare and watched as they effeminized society into being nothing more than a pair of massively-spread open legs, inviting in the lowest common denominator in the name of "tolerance". The whores of Babylon have bayed in the night and Western man has listened for generations from the shrinking comfort of his suburban existence.

This once great, gleaming society is undermined by the seedlings of the welfare state. Little remains now, just a mad grab for the scraps by those in power. The symphonies are dying away. All is becoming a rabble and still our man is pressed by the feminine, administrative state to remain tolerant. He must play nice with the foreigners lest he be placed in chains by the most brainwashed of his own kind. He will see dog meat served in the grocery stores. He will see big burly men penetrating his daughters. Still, he must hold his tongue lest he be a "racist".

The solution to the rising of the third worlders, which will decimate all high culture and society in the world, lies within Western man's remaining capacity for courage and assertiveness. He must reassert his place in this world. No longer may he sit idly in his private thoughts of "racism". He must now air those thoughts. The tide is not welcome upon his shores. He must snatch away the philosophical narrative from the globalists and their wicked welfare state. He must carefully note all the traitors from his tribe. He must reject the alien cultures thoroughly and totally. They are not welcome in his lands. He must reject fratricide forever. He must prepare himself for war to achieve peace through strength.

Psychology as the Replacement of Philosophy

Once upon a time, hardcore cocaine addict Sigmund Freud found out that his patients were being sexually abused. He made the link from this abuse to "hysteria" experienced in adulthood. He called this "seduction theory". Instead of sticking to the truth of the situation, he chose a more politically convenient position for himself by saying his clients' memories were instead fantasies[30]. Not only that but he claimed children were the seducers. Freud was a sick guy!

No one called Freud out on this until Florence Rush in the 1970's. Thousands of psychological theorists operated off of many of Sigmund Freud's founding principles in the eighty or so years after his deliberate cover up of sexual abuse in his clients[31]. As such, psychology departed from the realm of moral action into the realm of introspective avoidance of reality. The father of modern psychology was an extreme pervert! All who failed to account for this as they built upon his work have been non-actors in the actual, real work of improving the health of society: saving children from pedophiles and weeding pedophiles from the gene pool.

When we view Austrian-Jewish Sigmund Freud not as a "psychologist" but as a philosopher, we begin to understand that he was a man of incredible weakness, sickness, and deception. He used the relatively novel concept of systemizing one's own mental processes, to lead people away from the very crimes responsible for most problems in society. He was lionized by his contemporaries and by thousands of institutions of psychology in the 20th century. If he had not covered up the sexual crimes of Austrian high society, perhaps

---

[30]http://a.co/fVng7A3

[31]The only psychoanalytic theory still seems to hold water is the idea of "projection".

these people would have been brought to justice and we could have averted war!

Only now do we begin to see Sigmund Freud more clearly, with the standards of philosophy: a manipulative intellectual who spun baroque webs of non-actionable theory while living off the fat of the land of his day.

Other members of the European intelligentsia quickly learned that they too could get considerable government funding to experiment with the mental states of patients in government institutions. They used Freud's writings to institutionalize their ideas. Their work disseminated through the public schooling and university systems. Turns out that it's not *that* difficult to create vast, complex systems of self-masturbatory, non-market-oriented mental theory that gets people turning inward and away from the difficult moral questions of the day!

Bothered by someone who is able to draw great attention to himself in the free market?

Call him a malignant narcissist!

Threatened by someone who is skeptical of your vast, flowery language designed to paralyze him?

Call him a toxic abuser and a pathological coward!

Too cowardly to fight for improved conditions in your home country?

Claim "identity" is a tool of manipulation of the patriarchy and move around, living on the fat of the land like your psychological teachers did.

Frightened by the prospect of doing something other than living in your constant mental autism, like changing a diaper on a child you could have?

Claim that the family is a sick institution and to blame for all the neuroses of capitalism. There, now you don't have to reproduce!

Terrified by the prospect of having to put pedophiles to death with your own bare hands?

Claim that children are capable of consent and lose yourself in years of chasing down worthless degrees.

Psychology has not germinated in the free market. Modern psychology, by and large, is the dark art of turning people away from actionable moral questions in the here and now into whatever school of autism is most championed by the government-funded researchers de jure. Psychiatry goes a step further because it is not content with staying limited to verbal manipulation only. Its practitioners provoke chemical dependency in their clients. There are also academic "philosophers" who live off of the government and get lost into the same kinds of questions of minutiae that psychologists do. These turds aren't as dangerous as the licensed clinical mental health kind because they do not have the societal sanction of being "healers" of any kind. But they do participate in the brainwashing of the youth.

Free market philosophy is the answer to psychology. It is the brave and courageous men and women who operate fully in the free market that are positing the only complete solutions that will help society turn toward freedom and away from government intervention. Psychologists merely attend to the aberrant mental effects of expanding governments and invading foreign hordes. They claim they are working within "family systems" as if the best social program isn't simply a good job where one isn't serving the clawing hands of hungry, sexually frustrated Third Worlders! Questions of "psychology" will never be answered by people so timid of the free market they took out massive debts to operate in state cartels for their entire adult lives. Questions of "psychology" will be resolved by free market philosophers and businessmen who are the living embodiments of proactive, pro-social living geared toward resolving pertinent moral questions of the day.

Until the West rejects psychology and embraces philosophy, we will only continue to see pathetic neo-priests tending to the wounds of slaves bound to government whipping posts as the whips flay on and on. Psychologists are not the moral philosophers of our time.

Lifestyle Over Identity

Lifestyle, as defined by Dictionary.com, is:

the habits, attitudes, tastes, moral standards, economic level, etc., that together constitute the mode of living of an individual or group

In modern usage, the emphasis of the term "lifestyle" is on "mode of living", and has little to no bearing on the question of moral standards. As Western man has become detached from his history and moral center through the many sickening aspects of modernity, many theoreticians have stepped in to offer a solution: lifestyle.

The lifestyle industry is concerned with providing maximum ease and mental comfort to its customers. Lifestyle offers man a structure within which to frame his life, free of the concerns of history, morality, and tradition. Lifestylists work in the service of a globalist, cosmopolitan society wherein man gives up his roots and lives among a rabble, all the while trying to be efficient in his ease. Magazines touting quick fixes, exotic travel, new products, and new fad diets to make life easier have dominated the news stands for decades. Websites with beautiful, smiling idiots are sprouting up all the time, each of them offering viewers the chance at more ease.

The lifestylists work overtime to convince us that the only struggle we have is with ourselves and that a nice set of six pack abs will help us feel more "whole". Lifestylists deliberately sidestep questions of tribe with respect to genetics and cultural history in favor of concentration around activities and busywork.

Identity is *actually* concerned with the moral standards of an individual or group. Identity is the quality of moral, genetic, cultural-historical, and philosophical sameness between peoples. Questions of identity blow the lid off of the slow-crawling nihilism of consumerist, multicultural, welfare society. One comes to realize there are fundamental qualities that set him apart from peoples of other races, regardless of how fun yoga with Arjun was that afternoon[32]. One comes to realize the great damage multiculturalism does upon mixed-culture children. One comes to realize that once

---

[32]I studied yoga with slight Indian men in Vietnam for six months and loved it. It was a lot of fun, when I could understand what they were saying.

recessive traits are lost, they are lost for good. One sees that relentless multiculturalism reduces once proud and distinct peoples into the sediments of the ocean floor. This only serves to make people more pliable and controllable for a globalist, hyper elite administrative state, subsidized by Cheeseburger And Burrito America.

If the world turns toward philosophy, we can count on certain changes happening in society. Conflicts that previous generations avoided through "lifestyle[33]" will begin to erupt. Autonomy will begin to matter more than ever. Empathy will deepen as people begin to understand that shared philosophical, genetic, and cultural histories mentally shape members of the same tribe in a unique manner and in a way that few outsiders could ever grasp. The self-absorbed mantra of lifestylists will give way to a sense of belonging. Nihilism will recede, people will wake up, and suddenly there will be very real enemies standing in the way of freedom.

Deconstruction of the Family

The family unit is the backbone of society. The health of the family is the weakness of the state. Marxist strategists, driven by Saul Alinsky's Critical Theory,

---

[33]Boomers with powerboats purchased with credit cards. Yes, it's happened.

have been on the attack against the family unit since the feminist revolution. The elite are mortally threatened by the prospect of strong, Western men coming from wholesome families. These are the sort of men to bring the elite to justice for their crimes against humanity.

Hollywood media has been used as a propaganda arm of the international elite. Film after film over the 20th and 21st centuries have shown children in compromising moral and sexual positions. This serves to normalize the treatment of children as adults, a signal to end childhood and the precious value of innocence. Films such as *Taxi Driver* have depicted children as prostitutes. Films such as *The Lost Boys* and *Weird Science* show young men without guidance delving into the occult. Woody Allen married his stepdaughter. Roman Polanski raped a girl. Bryan Singer held naked boy pool parties. Harvey Weinstein masturbated into potted plants and pressured actresses into giving him blowjobs.

Nearly all Hollywood films show adults behaving wretchedly with no true, redeeming parental figures to counterbalance the toxicity. Cartoons dating back to *He-Man* are filled with Satanist programming or are filled with vapid, nihilistic characters who concern themselves with self-esteem, as opposed to morality. Shows such as *The Simpsons* and *Family Guy* depict patriarchs as bumbling buffoons and perverts. Shows such as *South Park* depict children as mini stoner-adults who have never been loved by their parents. Some of the newest fads in Hollywood include overemphasized multiculturalism, which erases a person's identity, such as in the forgettable film *A United Kingdom*. We also see Hollywood going out of its way to promote films that feature non-whites going through third world problems in an effort to drum up white sympathy, such as in the films *Lion* and *Moonlight*.

On the psychological side of things, those who seek to deconstruct the family unit preach that it is nothing more than a cult for perverse, power hungry parents to play their fantasies out onto the children. In order to suit their agenda, the deconstructionists will deliberately avoid questions of true parental love and the transmission of philosophical values over the generations. Family life is instead depicted as a prison for children. Endless stories of parental abuse clot their pages but nary an example of healthy families exist for them[34]. They underscore abuse as if it occurs at the hands of parents without outside influences.

Never mind the rampant taxation, forced integration of disparate and different peoples, or the

---

[34]http://a.co/1Tolsu8

sickening welfare state that morally withers grown adults. All questions regarding the family must be attributed to some deep neurosis that only the social metaphysician (psychologist) can deconstruct. These psychological wizards quietly harbor delusions of being saviors, "If only the world would listen to me! I have all the answers. It's trauma and trauma alone!". On and on they attack the family from the confines of their state cartels and inculcate their own children, those who do have them, with the same denial of economics and the marketplace they harbor.

The deconstruction of the family has been institutionalized through government food stamps, unemployment benefits, single-parent subsidies, child "protective" services, and the university system which harbors an anti-traditional intelligentsia.

Food stamps programs take money from producers in the free market and puts it into the hands of non-producers. This is highly dysgenic. Smart people forced to pay for dumb people to breed. Unemployment rewards people for not working and subsidizes their laziness and ineptitude. Single-parent subsidies ensure that people who make poor partner choices are rewarded for their idiocy and inability to keep a stable marriage.

Child protective services routinely sell children off to child traffickers to be used as sex slaves and anyone who investigates it is killed off. Government is the primary destroying force of the family because its predations have legal and moral sanction in the land whereas psychological theories and mass media often do not. It is much more dangerous and inadvisable to resist a kidnapper working under the guise of "child protection" than it is to simply shut off the TV or avoid going to university.

To restore the family institution to prominence, moral philosophers in the free market must be willing to adopt or adapt the Alinsky tactics and use them against the leftists. Fire can fight fire. By burning out boundary lines in the ground, people will be able to put an end to the spread of leftism. The family can be defended but only if its assailants are disabled. The left has no arguments, only derision. A philosophical person can do derision better than the Cultural Marxists because philosophy is grounded in unshakeable principles that make Marxists crap their pants.

Meme warfare is spicy precisely because it hurts Marxists where they already hurt. These family-abusers have no ammunition left other than to squelch free speech. They are a dying breed, but they still hold dangerous positions of power in the West. To finish them off we need to simply keep pouring on the precision point meme deluge. The art of leftism is corny and passé. The psychological purview of leftism is limited and stumpy. Government programs that smash up families are outdated, inefficient, and horrific. We, the people, need to simply repeat these truths with the spiciest memes we can imagine and social consensus will do the rest. Enough people will catch on and society will change. There is no turning back. Of course, the point is to pour it on so thick that public school intellectual programming is vaporized from people's minds.

Young people and children *love* memes. What better way to fight the deconstruction of the family than to adopt a format that is family friendly?

Flattening of Social Hierarchies

This aspect of modernity has been enforced largely by anti-discrimination laws. In a freer society with a strong middle class, social groups form around the financial or social prowess of competent men and women. These social groups can enter the marketplace and generally perform services that benefit the immediate community. The cohesion of these groups is greatly aided by identity. Identity allows for easy empathy between group members, allowing them to follow the steady lead of the most competent members. Anti-discrimination laws forcibly integrate people that would otherwise not be permitted into certain groups, namely the longstanding fraternal societies of the majority. This has a corroding effect on voluntary social groups, particularly those who have entered the marketplace to benefit the community in one way or another.

The primary and traditional champions of community associations and social groups benefitting the West have been White Anglo-Saxon Protestants (WASPS). With their fraternal organizations, women's groups, churches, private schools, and country clubs, the WASPS were the backbone of the broader culture of independence, family values, and upward mobility in the United States. With the WASPS at the helm of American society, all other groups in the United States were able to find their footing in one way or another and assimilate into the West.

The Civil Rights Act of 1964 and the Voting Rights Act of 1965, both signed into law by black-hating President Lyndon Baines Johnson[35], undid the social hierarchy that was so necessary to America's success. Rather than seek a principled repeal of legal segregation

---

[35]"I'll have those niggers voting Democratic for the next 200 years," LBJ once said with respect to his Great Society welfare programs.

at the state level, leftist activists ensured that America would be forced by compulsion to be inclusive. The wording of these acts betrays a ruse wherein "discrimination", a voluntary choice on the part of private citizens, was outlawed. More than the banning of legal racism from government institutions, choice itself was removed from the private and business lives of Americans. Choice is an internal function based on volition and conscience.

By legally enforcing inclusion beyond the scope of government institutions, a change that targeted the social hierarchy of the United States, the leftists operating within the United States ensured that minorities would be forcibly included in the traditional community associations. This would erode and flatten social hierarchies, destroy the efficacy of private institutions, and result in the massive expansion of government intervention in the markets. Given the propensity of the "Greatest Generation" to follow orders from above due to WWII boot camp brainwashing, WASPS had a massive hand in their own decimation from the social order by practicing inclusion when other peoples would not.

Foreign people have largely ignored the inclusion mandate in the decades since and have succeeded in building alternate societies where their values, prejudices, and languages have flourished compared to the dutiful self-oblivion of WASPS. Foreigners have not played by the rules. Minority victimhood[36], a lie introduced to the public schools by leftist theorists in academia and the Department of Education, has given further license to foreigners to ignore the inclusion mandate.

Western man cannot hold higher standards than those who seek his exclusion or even his destruction. He is not allowed to bring his exclusive associations into the marketplace without facing a deluge of greedy lawyers screaming, "discrimination" on behalf of cultural foreigners. He can still practice a modicum of freedom of association in his private, social life. He can choose to associate primarily or only with members of his own tribe and pursue non-commercial means of advancing the interests of his people. This is possible because Western man still has free speech assurances in the United States.

It is the place of intelligent people to remind less intelligent people of their standing, from time to time. Those of us who remember the glories of WASP institutions in the United States have the chance to use our free speech to remind those who would trade their freedoms for political correctness of the value of

---

[36]http://a.co/60Xb7Xj

freedom of association across the institutions. Cultures that have not germinated in conditions of freedom cannot compete in fair market conditions with the standards the WASPS were able to bring to bear for 188 years. They have to use the violence of the state. Now, more than ever, it is important to uphold the standards once freely available to us as we wage the battle against globalists. Eventually we will undo the laws that favor foreign cultures so intensely.

Social hierarchy in the West will rise again but only if Western man fights to regain his freedom to choose.

The West was founded and built by Western man. It is up to him to awaken from the stupor of the World Wars and find his fighting spirit once again. It is in his best interests to negate the failures of non-Western cultures in bringing the world a prosperous society. It is in his best interests to shake off the self-loathing chains of the welfare state and remediate his family values. And only Western man can convince the women of his tribe to take up these values and deny global Communism its final victory.

What's Good These Days

This is an essay to compliment and contrast against the essay "The Madness of Modernity". We're out of the ugly neck of the woods, for the time being. Let's look at the world from a different point of view. What has technology brought us? What are the things to be celebrated in the modern world? What is genuinely improving and why?

Homeschooling

Thanks to the proliferation of the Internet, homeschooling is on the rise. Between 1999 and 2007, the rate of homeschooling rose roughly 50%, adjusted for population growth[37]. Homeschooling in the United States entered the national conversation in the 1980's and has since been legalized in all 50 states, to one degree or another. Homeschooling is to be celebrated as public schooling serves as little more than a leftist indoctrination camp.

Public school is where children are policed for their language, teachers regularly have sex with their underage students[38], children of different races are

---

[37]https://theconversation.com/heres-how-homeschooling-is-changing-in-america-63175

[38]https://www.washingtonpost.com/news/education/wp/2017/11/1

lumped in together leading to massive brawls and increased militarization of school authorities[39], and where curriculum often remains hopelessly outdated. Seriously, who needs to learn German anymore? You're better served learning Arabic or Somali.

Homeschooling leaves education in the hands of parents, those most incentivized to ensure their children are economically and socially functional as adults. Public school teachers have vanishing pensions and resentful children to rely on in old age. Homeschooling parents give their family line a much better chance at success by sparing their children from the collectivized ills of public schooling.

The best homeschooling is the kind that has structure, rigor, play, and market viability. With structure, children learn that reality can be systematized and that they will be rewarded the more consistency they introduce into their learning process. Rigor challenges children to accept more and more responsibility. By accepting more responsibility, children can rise in social hierarchies and spread more goodwill, wealth, and truth throughout the world. Play allows children to synthesize their learning experiences

---

0/teacher-admits-to-having-sex-with-her-students-and-sending-nude-photos-on-snapchat-police-say/

[39]https://www.amazon.com/Dont-Make-Black-Kids-Angry/dp/1508585024

through physical interaction with their environment. Play encourages exploration, bodily joy, and spontaneity, all vital aspects of becoming a sociable, enterprising person. Market viability is the responsibility of the parent: to teach the child skills and principles that will allow them to enter the marketplace as a young person and maintain sustainable employment.

One could argue, "Well, Steven, homeschooling existed broadly before public schooling!" I'd have to agree. The main points of difference between now and the 1880's (do I even need to outline them?) are that young people have more choice than ever before, infant mortality rate is way down, and the Internet is a Pandora's Box of learning. Parents and children are better equipped for education success in the home. We are not living in the time of, "blacksmith father trains a blacksmith son". We are in an economy that is more like, "a car salesman father trains a son in sales and then the son sells...crypto currency services!"

Parenting is Improving

Slowly but surely it is entering the public eye that hitting children as a punishment is literally a stupid thing to do. Research by Murray Strauss, a professor at University of New Hampshire, shows that, "IQs of children ages 2 to 4 who were not spanked were 5 points higher four years later than the IQs of those who were spanked[40]." If you have a kid that is set to have the average IQ of Americans in later life, 98, the choice of whether you spank or not could be the difference for your child of whether they will be a welfare dependent their whole lives or work some meaningful career contributing to the lives of others.

Hitting children is barbaric even aside from the IQ drop involved. Children who learn to resolve conflict with violence go on to adult lives where they apply this lesson. They may risk prison time, divorce, death in foreign conflicts, lost jobs, and nearly endless other complications and dysfunctions as adults. They will be that awkward adult in the room who is all too eager for conflict to escalate since, after all, they were programmed to be this way in childhood. They will be more susceptible to lower cultures than the reason and enlightenment culture of the West. They will be happy, at times, to trade a little bit of philosophy for a little bit of violence. And if you just so happen to have a kid with the Warrior Gene or the Wandering Gene, beating them as children for being incapable of reasoning at an adult level could turn them into career freak-outs or perpetual drifters. Not a good choice.

---

[40]http://scholars.unh.edu/cgi/viewcontent.cgi?article=1204&context=news

Clubbing a child with your fists or a shoe or a belt is pure idiocy. More and more people are understanding this because they go on the Internet and encounter thinkers and creators who cannot possibly sustain violence in their personal lives and still maintain platforms. The days of Legacy Media where you could be a literal sociopath, get trained by the CIA, party with sex cults on the weekends, and have a regular hosting gig on CNN are coming to an end. The standards for what it means to be a disseminator of knowledge have risen.

With the Trumpian advent of crackdowns on human trafficking, child trafficking and prostitution, and what could potentially be proven to be ritual mutilation and sacrifice of children by the global elite, we will see a shift in public discourse on what is acceptable treatment of children. All it will take is, say, one brave person at the FBI willing to risk their life by leaking a video of a global celebrity raping a child and the whole house of cards will come tumbling down. The days where leftist, degenerate "comedians" can make jokes about having sex with dead children[41] without public ostracism are coming to an end. The culture is changing. Kids matter more than ever. Eventually standards will rise to the point where children will be

---

[41]Louis CK

able to signal to outsiders, via some sort of notification platform, whether they are being spanked in the home or not. Other such improvements are on the way. We only need imagine and then act.

Women are Staying Home

Marxist deconstruction of Western traditionalism, via feminism in this case, has basically run its course. The false glitz and glamour of entering the workforce has worn off for women. Women in the workplace drives down wages, leads to marital dissatisfaction, and strains the mother-child bond. Many women choose to persist in the workplace with rationalizations such as, "I can be a great mom *and* maintain a full time career" or "My mother worked and I turned out *just fine*". When you ask these women about their standards, they become evasive and self-justifying. As knowledge of the value of stay at home moms continues to disseminate, more and more women will transition to the home.

Some people, confused by the public schooling they went through and the lies told to them at university, have not made the financial planning necessary to transition the woman in the home. Having empathy for these people is not the same as condoning the strain they put on their children through their absence, use of babysitters, daycare and extended family, and the message of basic neglect they put on their children.

The upside of women staying home is marketed marvelously via social media by women such as Aaryn Williams, Hayley Paige, VasseurBeauty, and Wife With A Purpose. The upside is that the *whole family* is happier with mother at home. A woman's natural role is to nurture, multi-task in service of the household, and to act as a secondary protector when the man is away. There are women who are outliers to this rule, for various and not always rational reasons, but the trend is that women are choosing to belong in the home. Children love knowing that mother is there to feed them and love them when they need. "Spoiling" a child actually has a lot more to do with shipping a child off to public school to consume crappy government food and interact with over-sexualized television victims than it has to do with having a loving mother around to cook home cooked meals and learning at home.

Fathers are happier with the mother at home because it encourages, neigh, forces them to earn at higher rates. Men are cut out for swashbuckling in the marketplace. They are emasculated by wives who out earn them simply because hiring "womyn" is the hot thing to do right now. Fathers love coming home to a tidy home and a home cooked meal. They love being greeted by children who got enough attention throughout the day. They love shouldering the financial responsibility of being accountable to dependents. They have much less time to slide into video games, substances, under employment, and political discontent.

Women savor the confidence gained by pursuing a natural born role. In the best of households they are free to fashion a warm, inviting atmosphere where they glide along as keen hostesses. They take pride in such pursuits as sewing, canning, cleaning, and sometimes accounting. With the love of a good husband they are empowered to have a symbiotic stake in the only true institution of equality: marriage.

The man who fails to help his woman get "back in the kitchen" is a weaker man, much more exposed to the blowing winds of leftism. Not to mention the strain a two career household has on a marriage.

Philosophy is Gaining Ground

Man's technology is driven by philosophical advances. Scientism is the point of view that progress is made only through the improvement of science. Philosophers know that scientists quietly look to them for inspiration and insight. I could name plenty of gizmos and gadgets that have made people die less and live longer but beneath each technology lie philosophical assumptions. Essentially, people want to love another more fully. Science serves the progress in this ever complexifying conversation. It is not the other way around.

The Internet is populated with thinkers such as Stefan Molyneux, Styxhexenhammer666, and Sargon of Akkad offering philosophical commentary on world events. We are seeing celebrities such as Roseanne Barr, Kanye West, and James Woods offer honest perspectives. Anyone with an open mind and a few IQ points to rub together is getting exposed to argumentation and logic at an unprecedented scale.

Whether humanity advances civilization through this cycle of history or not remains to be seen. There is much to celebrate in this day and age. Only extraordinary effort will put humanity over the top. We all do well to support truth speakers in every conceivable way.

Lift Weights

The seven benefits of regular physical activity according to the Mayo Clinic are[42]:

1. Exercise controls weight (by boosting your metabolism)

2. Exercise combats health conditions and diseases (by boosting your immune system and increasing circulation)

3. Exercise improves mood (by releasing endorphins in your system)

4. Exercise boosts energy (by delivering more oxygen and nutrients to your tissues)

5. Exercise promotes better sleep

6. Exercise raises libido

7. Exercise can be fun and social

Here are my five reasons for lifting weights:

1. Increased confidence -

You need confidence to stand up to the power elite, the brain dead Left, and endless foreigners. To be able to say, "This is the line in the sand and you are not passing." There is no one successfully waging the

---

[42]http://www.mayoclinic.org/healthy-lifestyle/fitness/in-depth/exercise/art-20048389

culture war who does not have some measure of confidence. Lifting weights can make a huge difference.

Increased confidence allows you to voice the difficult truths our Western society has been so long in denial about. Confidence makes you more persuasive, charming, and loveable. Lifting weights does not necessarily mean you transform into a horrible brute who treats others poorly, though some of those types may be necessary. You can use your increased physique in the service of becoming a salesman and philosopher-king.

2. Sexual market value –

"Have not just three but five children," President Erdogan of the 99.8% Muslim majority Turkey recently told Turkish citizens residing in Europe[43]. Muslims will have an easy time at reproducing because their culture and societies have not been infected by the cancer of feminism. Their sky high, consanguineous marriage rates ensure that the majority of them look like twice baked potatoes[44]. Muslim men have little to no barrier to entry to the sexual market, among their own kind. Yet, Islam is ugly.

---

[43]http://www.telegraph.co.uk/news/2017/03/17/erdogan-calls-turkish-families-have-five-children-bulwark-against/
[44]https://wikiislam.net/wiki/Cousin_Marriage_in_Islam

Thanks to feminist indoctrination, ethnic Westerners have a whole lot of pomp and circumstance to go through. Looking cut as a cage fighter will significantly increase the chances of netting yourself a recovering cat lady maiden and then making babies with her. You may even draw the attention of higher sexual market value women if you keep at it long enough. Lifting weights makes you look more manly and dominant. Women are hardwired to feel arousal at the sight of a hulking, well-groomed muscle man.

3. Preparedness –

Depending on your locale, ethnic clashes may or may not break out in your lifetime. Those of us in the American West have it much better than those in Sweden. The element of preparedness in an increasingly multicultural world cannot be understated. The Muslims know this. They have tons of boxing clubs in Europe where they train with weights and gloves while eating huge omelets, all subsidized by ethnic European taxpayers. They know "what's up". We Westerners will have to get with the program if we expect to outlast them once they do something truly stupid like blowing up the Eiffel Tower or taking over military bases from which to command the surrounding region. There will be ethnic clashes in the streets. You are going to need muscle and training to defend yourself against attackers. Muscle will help you to defend yourself against the Sharia police that will come to your home to drag you off to your new home in a forced labor camp.

4. Discipline and Structure –

Ethnic conflict aside, having some muscle on your bones will signal to other Western men that you are physically capable. A muscular man is an inspiring sight for any man who still has some martial instincts left in him. Physical fitness signifies order, structure, regimen, and discipline. These are martial traditions. A man who is of the martial traditions is a man who can be relied upon to serve his fellow man much more than noodle-armed men who TV talk and inhabit a soy bean world. Building muscle requires personal sacrifice and dedication. Civilization rewards those who practice these virtues.

5. We Are Descended from Hunter-Gatherers –

As Mark Sisson writes in his blog, *Mark's Daily Apple*, "The hunter-gatherers' daily energy expenditures for physical activity typically were at least 800 to 1200 kcal or about 3 to 5 times that of modern sedentary individuals[45]." Our forefathers, as agriculturalists predating the industrial revolution, were massively

---

[45]http://www.marksdailyapple.com/the-characteristics-of-hunter-gatherer-fitness/)

active compared to most people today. Our forefathers predating the agricultural revolution, as hunter-gatherers, were busy running around, trying to survive. They concerned themselves with intense physical activity in order to eke out lives. They had higher testosterone and fertility levels than us[46]. Even their leisure time was spent in physical play. They evolved to be lean, out of necessity, and light on their feet.

Our modern day bodies operate best when we honor their physical routines. We are not meant to be sitting most of every day, watching television as Muslims pour into the West. Our genetic inheritance is to be active and mobile. We do well to respect our nature as human beings. Show up to the gym and let your body do the talking. Everyone is a natural fit for it. Not everyone will let themselves do the hard work. It's time to separate the wheat from the chaff.

Perspectives: Julian Langness pt. 1
twitter.com/J_Langness

---

[46]https://ifstudies.org/blog/baby-bust-fertility-is-declining-the-most-among-minority-women

Julian is the author of several books, including *Identity Rising* and *The Coming War In Europe*. He is a regular contributor to Counter Currents and has spoken at the American Renaissance conference. He also maintains a YouTube channel titled Conquering Modernity. His focuses include masculinity, fourth generation warfare, and political philosophy.

Why should all men be lifting weights?

All men should lift weights because all men should be strong. We, as men, evolved to be physically strong- it's at the very core of what makes us men- as evidenced by the fact that superior strength is one of the defining differences between men and women. Our ancestors had to be physically strong in order to protect their families and tribes, just to be able to survive.

Today, however, our hyper-efficient societies have outsourced strength and violence to a tiny, tiny percentage of men, which means that the other 99.9% can afford to be weak and effeminate and soft. These qualities are even celebrated, while traditional masculine attributes such as strength are denigrated as being part of "toxic masculinity". Ironically, the only reason such naïve, destructive thinking can exist today is because of the overwhelming strength of our ancestors, and the immense sacrifices they made to ensure our people's survival.

-If we aren't as strong as we can be, we dishonor those ancestors.

-If we aren't a strong as we can be, sooner or later another man will have to pick up our slack.

-If we aren't strong as we can be, sooner or later we won't be able to protect our families.

Exercising strength and doing everything we can to continually improve our strength is thus the ultimate validation of life, and the total rejection of nihilism.

Why are young men depressed and what are your recommendations for them to improve?

Some level of depression is a part of the human condition. We may be able to worry more about our "depression" today since we're not getting chased around by sabre-tooth tigers, but that doesn't mean our ancestors didn't feel the same thing. Conversely though, it's likely that that very absence of threats that has added to the levels of "depression" seen today. Danger, death, pain, and suffering have a way of making you unbelievably grateful for anything that doesn't involve them, and the fact that we have made society so safe and secure and painless probably causes a lot of existential angst, especially among men. That doesn't mean safety and security are bad things- just that it's a dynamic we should be aware of.

Depression among men today is also the result of low testosterone levels. If you have low testosterone you are drastically, drastically more likely to suffer from depression and anxiety. The two things overlap to about an 80% degree in my estimation.

Men are also depressed because they are consuming rather than creating. Playing video games, watching pornography, watching movies, watching television, watching pro sports, eating food, drinking soda, drinking alcohol, taking drugs... these are all manners of consumption, and they all- to varying degrees- lead to bad things when they are consumed in anything but the most extreme moderation.

Writing, lifting weights, building things, tinkering with cars, collecting stamps or tropical fish or gold coins, making new friends, farming, cooking food, starting businesses, having children... these are all forms of creation, and all lead to very good things.

Men today consume far more than they create however, and the former activities are far more common than the latter.

Part of this is just the result of technological innovation, which has allowed addictive forms of consumption to be far more powerful and far more readily available than at any time in the past.

Part of it is also that it is often far easier to monetize things that are consumed. Because of this there are lots of people trying to get you to consume things so they can make money, whereas no one is really out there trying to convince you to build a birdhouse or write a song. This isn't always a bad thing, again some consumption in moderation is okay, buts it's important to keep in mind so that you remember to create far more than you consume.

By focusing on building one's strength, by focusing on being a man of integrity and decency, and by focusing on creating rather than consuming, I think the average man can drastically reduce the likelihood of depression afflicting him, or overcome it if it is.

What is the essence of masculinity and why does it matter?

I never thought about this question until I was about 26-27 years old, and stumbled upon the writings of Brett McKay (editor of artofmanliness.com) and Jack Donovan (author of The Way of Men[47]).

Their writings on this subject were a splash of cold water to the face, and had a tremendously positive impact on me. I still think they provide the two best definitions of masculinity I've found:

-Brett McKay says that masculinity is based upon the three-pronged mission he calls "Protect, Procreate, and Provide".

-Jack Donovan says that masculinity is based upon the four tactical masculine virtues of "Strength, Courage, Mastery, and Honor".

I think the two men are saying basically the same thing, and both stress the fact that masculinity is defined by its amoral nature. What this means it that morality and masculinity are distinct things.

---

[47]http://a.co/icdgIOS

A good, moral man can be either masculine or un-masculine (effeminate), and a bad, immoral man can also be either masculine or un-masculine.

There is a difference between being a "good man" and being someone who is "good at being a man" which is another way of saying "masculine".

To be good at being a man you must be possessed of high qualities of the aforementioned masculine "tactical virtues" of strength, courage, mastery, and honor.

Strenuousness without virtue is dangerous, and so is virtuousness without strenuousness.

Some of our ancestors- admittedly- had lots of strenuousness but little virtuousness. On the opposite side, many men today seek to constantly prove their virtuousness through "virtue-signaling"; are effeminate; and reject masculinity. They want to be virtuous without being strenuous (although really they are neither).

As men alive in today's world, I believe we should strive to be both. We should work hard at being a "good man" and also work towards being "good at being a man".

Shock The System

"I'd always try to shock the muscles...This shocking method was extremely important to my training. Your muscles tend to become complacent and resist growth if you are constantly doing the same workout for them. But if you try all different types of training methods, exercises, weights, set-rep combinations and training tempos, you keep the muscles off balance."

-Arnold Schwarzenegger

I have written extensively about the pursuit of self-knowledge in my books and blogs over the years. I have advocated for the journaling–plus-self-reflection approach to getting to know oneself better. You do sentence completions and general prompts, probe and comb over your many years with an eye to empathize with who you were at some stage in life, and simply sit and ponder. This is a worthwhile use of time, particularly for those who feel like large chunks of their time is spent playing Whack-A-Mole with their endless thoughts. Slowing down and getting out of your head and into your body yields all sorts of good stuff.

However, there are some who pursue this kind of self-excavation at the expense of having actual lives.

The "Self-Knowledge Zone" becomes a place of comfort to retreat to if life becomes scary. For these people there is always one more stone to turn over. Their lives become a never ending set of self-centered musings while the society around them marches on.

I can guarantee you: Muhammad and Muhammad Jr. don't think this way. No, the Muslim hordes invading the West are not so sensitive. The globalist elite unleashing these hordes are not so sensitive either. From their point of view, there is conquering to be done and children to be had. They do as much with little to no quibbling.

If those who are interested in knowing themselves better don't show up for the major contests in life, those of political and genetic hegemony, personal sensitivity will be bred out of the gene pool. You can't live your little apartment life, turn on Internet videos or your journal every time you're afraid of going out and living, and expect to have any influence in today's society. You have to go out and live!

The ivory tower is temporary, as I mentioned in a previous book. The time young men and women spend in the ivory tower is paid for by the political, economic, and genetic advances of our Western forefathers. The ivory tower is *only* appropriate for people in their teens and early 20's. By the time those mid-20's roll around, you better be getting into that culture war and buying time for future generations or you can expect your civilization to dry up real fast. If you are in your late 20's or 30's and still trying to "find yourself", what you're doing isn't serving you. You'll need to shock the system.

It is shocking to leave your ivory tower, isn't it? You'll get over it. Young American men enlisted as 14 year olds in the Revolutionary War, knocked the hell out of the British, and went on to start whole industries. Right now there is an invasion of the West. Buckle up, bud. You are needed for something greater than yourself.

There are a nihilistic few, often known as "psychologists", who will go into their 30's, 40's, 50's, and so forth thinking they're "finding themselves". They didn't do it right. Finding your purpose in life doesn't take all that long, particularly if you read my previous books. Your purpose in life is greater than yourself. It's not to try to manifest your own personal, artistic myth of superiority through some grand magnum opus that you craft from the confines of your ivory tower. That's just personal cowardice masquerading as genius.

No, you are here to advance civilization. You are here because strong men and women came before you. They carved out hard, grizzly lives to allow The Greatest

Generation to be tricked by globalists into fratricide on an industrial scale. They carved out hard, grizzly lives so that Baby Boomers could vote for massive government expansion and act like a bunch of entitled moralizers. Grizzly lives so that Millennials could zone out over Bernie Sanders and vagina jokes printed under the caps of soylent drinks. The buck stops with you, culture warrior. It's up to you to shock the system. It's up to you to let go of being an autist and actually do something that will make things better for Western people.

To the young men I say: take some time and get to know yourself better. Make mistakes, learn hard skills, journal and self-reflect, and keep your dick out of crazy.

To the grown men I say: you need to contribute.

The third world will steamroll you if you don't.

Two Betas Don't Make An Alpha

You may not know it but you could be a beta.

There is nothing particularly wrong with being a beta, so long as you have an alpha around. Everyone can cultivate for themselves the qualities of an alpha but that doesn't mean that everyone will. Nor does it mean that some men, simply because they make the effort, will automatically *become* alphas. There are betas. It is what it is.

Many, many betas try to compensate for their lack of alpha status by finding other betas to band together with. This is a step in the right direction. But it is not enough. If they don't want to lose their civilization, betas must be willing to seek out alphas, learn the ropes of becoming alphas themselves, and contribute to the culture war wherever they are at in the hierarchy.

It is in the psychological programming of betas to lean on other betas. This is a much needed trait when it comes to raising children but it is not a free pass for not having to grow up. It's not open season on cartoon watching and fart joking as a group. The prospect of being "more alpha" for the beta is an opportunity to learn more self-sufficiency, assertiveness, forthrightness, courage, and dependability.

Many betas think they can overcome their lack of alpha qualities by cloistering away into beta groups. They spot an alpha on the horizon and rather than come to him in the hopes of building a tribe, they pull away. They gossip like clucking hens, quick to point out the things they don't like in the alpha. They prefer the safety of their echo chambers. They don't feel "judged" in their degenerate habits. They think they are safe from the alpha. They reason that together they are equal to or superior to the alpha. This is not true. It's also worth noting that some beta men stay in their safe spaces with their beta female partners, suckling on feigned compassion and too much sex.

Betas who avoid alphas will be the first to be preyed upon by the out-groups when conflict goes down. Rather than develop themselves in a martial manner, learning the alpha ropes, they have spent their time degenerating. This makes them weak and flaccid. All their long nights of video games, gossip, and fast food will not spare them from the conflicts of the world.

This is not the way to live. This isn't even what can be considered a social life. These men need to find themselves. The going will be tough, but the tough have to get going. Either they pay the price by reforming themselves or their children will. It's simple. Some will choose to forgo having children all together. These men are "going their own way" when in actuality they are heeding the whims of the global elite that rule over them. It's in the best interests of Western men to reproduce because having a family gives a man unending purpose and a reason to die for the right cause.

Even if you consider yourself an alpha, there is always going to be someone who is more alpha than you, unless you are Donald Trump. You can always up your alpha game. Beware the betas who hold no aspirations. They are weak. They or their children will be cannon fodder. The betas who hold onto their aspirations will make themselves known to you. Every now and then one will reveal himself to be a natural alpha. Others will have to struggle to learn the ways of alphas. Often these are the men who did not have a strong father figure growing.

Not everyone *has* to be an alpha. To "become alpha" is aspirational. Some men are content to be betas. So long as they are not the avoidant kind of beta, they will find a way of contributing. Betas are useful, just not when they are in the habit of lying to themselves.

Liking or Respecting People

The job that needs to be done is for the mainstream to be discredited, disassembled, and destroyed in the minds of the general public. This is the most difficult endeavor in the history of mankind and the stakes are final. There will never again be this kind of opportunity to blow open the channels of communication and reach the masses with truth. The major social media platforms are scrambling to form alliances with the ADL, NAACP, and a bevy of NGO's so they can police or throttle all original thought out of the public conscience.

Given this struggle as the backdrop, we all need to form working relationships in order to advance freedom by making the best use of our abilities. There is a point of distinction I think a lot of people get confused on. I have been confused on it myself and want to offer my thoughts as a way of helping others to get going more efficiently than I have been able to.

There are people you like and people you respect. Sometimes you experience both of these at the same time, but rarely so.

Let's start with what merits respect.

Results merit respect. The results that matter in this war are twofold: who can do the most damage to the opposition and who can recruit the most capable people into the fray.

In this manner, respect is objective. In a weird way, we are in a popularity contest to the death with the globalist elite. No rational, reasonable person would choose these conditions for mankind. We are in a crap sandwich brought on by greed, apathy, and violence.

These forces have shaped our world into what it is now. Anyone with an idea of how society would ideally be maintains a level of dissatisfaction with the state of affairs but not at the expense of pursuing the two main, respectable strategies. Having traveled a bit in influential circles, I can guarantee there is a general awareness on the part of platformers of what "ought" to be as opposed to how things are at this point in time. This does not negate what needs to be done, it only informs us of longer term trajectory in strategy.

You can think of who scores "gotchas" against the media elite and those who rebut their talking points on a continual basis. You can also think of those brave warriors on the legalistic end who are undoing the lawsuits and defamation by the Left against freedom fighters, often themselves counter-suing. There are also whistle-blowers and populist politicians to think of. These are the forces doing the most damage against the opposition.

You can also think of teachers and thinkers who give insights to the masses, who convey the reasons for fighting for freedom. These people are vital. They often perform double duties and go on the offensive against the Left. These people are from all walks of life. Some are entertainers with legacy platforms they are cashing in on. Some are misfits who take their killer wit to

Twitter. Some are philosophical powerhouses who teach us about the good in life.

These are the people to respect. They achieve results. Results are the bottom line.

The people you like are a bit different. If you have firmly aligned your aesthetic standards for liking people to solely those who achieve results, my hat's off to you. Most people experience the people they like differently.

Broadly speaking, people we like are those who get us to feel pleasant feelings or remind us of how things used to be. Sometimes we like a composer who creates beauty but has no agenda to join in the fray. Perhaps this composer is long gone. Sometimes the person we like provided us with excellent service. Sometimes the person we like appeals to some level of comfort we need in the face of this overwhelming, all-encompassing battle for civilization's soul. Everyone contributes in some manner to the downward or upward movement of human consciousness but some simply are not cued into the tangible structure of the war being waged right now. Some are content to pursue their interests and not plug in too closely with the generals in the war.

We like our neighbor. We like our grocery bagger. We like our landscapers. We like our dentist. These people are not direct culture warriors, but they do brighten our days.

When considering results, it is important to untether your tendency to try respect someone from your general approval and liking of them as people. You may like people for the wrong reasons. Or you may like them and they are of little consequence to what really matters. If you want results, you are better off shaping your tendency to "like" toward your experience of genuine respect, not the other way around. Just because you like someone doesn't mean they are objectively respectable.

It is hard to like some people who are worthy of respect. Perhaps they are too this or that for your taste. If you can keep the like/respect distinction in mind, you will remain a more effective culture warrior. You do not have to like people to respect them.

Mommy

One term that floats around in psychology here and there that has made some sense to me over the years is the idea of a "rescue fantasy". It is a scenario or situation a person puts themselves in that replicates dynamics from their childhood. In this situation a person is either attempting to rescue someone else or to be rescued themselves as a primitive attempt to resolve the trauma of the dynamics of their childhood.

The most glaring example of this that I see on a near continual basis can be found in the way men choose to go about dating. I'm sure this happens to women just as often, only my focus for the past few years has been on men so I will speak to that foremost.

It is common for men to portray themselves as servile, adorable, eager to please, and "nerdy" in an attempt to elicit the mothering instinct from the women they are hoping to date. They need a mommy to make their boo-boo's feel better. We could turn away from such behavior in disgust and lampoon these guys, but many of them genuinely don't know any better. This was the way they gained sympathy from girls in public school. This is the way they got attention from their mothers.

The man who instead acts a rescuer puts on an equally fake act but gets more social approval for it. He needs women to know he is romantically tough, he especially emphasizes that he will not ever let them tell him what to do and will punish them if they try, and he acts in a manner that is cut off from his true feelings in order to achieve an idealized version of himself. Such a man often acts as a perverted father to a daughter, ultimately leaving women feeling exposed, debased, and punished after a brief and intense romance.

Both postures help a man prevent himself from experiencing vulnerable, unpleasant things from his history. He does not have to self-reflect and the roles of his romance are set up to operate predictably.

Breaking out of the rescue fantasy in order to attain true romance is not all that complicated. It requires self-reflection and empathy for the experiences of others. A man who cared about these things would ask for outside feedback and would gauge the effect his online profile had on women. The online profile is a fairly accurate representation of his actual personality with respect to dating. What kind of experience do women have of his profile and dating behaviors? Do they feel pity and soon click away? Do they salivate like Saint Bernards and daydream of love bombs? Or do they feel calm and encouraged to connect with their values and hopes for life?

Speaking to the needs, interests, and values of another person while remaining true to yourself is a process that requires a genuine interest and investment in the outcomes. You have to know what love is good for. It is not good for rescue. It is not good for posturing or acting pathetic. It will never redeem your childhood deficits. Romance is good for pair bonding, raising a family, and contributing to civilization. Most anything else is a distraction and will not serve a couple.

If you are looking for a babysitter who will suck your dick, be more honest with yourself and either grow up or hire a prostitute. If you are looking for a helpless daughter to molest while telling yourself you are a hero, grow up or try getting yourself a mail order bride from the Third World. Neither side of the rescue you put into your romantic pursuits will ever serve you in becoming a more rational, reasonable, and relatable person. You are going to have to choose the sophistication that self-reflection brings.

A dysfunctional relationship to women can make the difference as to whether you rise in the hierarchy or stay stuck at some level. Some men's entire lives are ruined because they're too love drunk to see they're just seeking another mommy.

Perspectives: Bre Faucheux

twitter.com/Bre_Faucheux

brefaucheux.com

Bre Faucheux is a popular YouTuber best known for her punchy videos exposing the hypocrisy of leftist elites.

-How can nationalist men redpill the women they care about? What helps in the process?

My suggestion would be to start pointing out fallacies within media narratives. If your woman pays attention to news cycles, point out how the media clearly takes a side and has their own narrative that they're trying to push. Whether that be how anti-white they are, or how many news outlets are Far Left, or if you're really brave, point out how they're predominantly owned by globalists with foreign interests.

If your woman isn't particularly interested in politics, you can point out smaller things that might directly impact her life. Does she complain about traffic and commuting to work? Well, immigration is largely to blame for that with the large influx of people in recent decades. Does she want a higher paying job? Well, immigrants, particularly illegal ones, bring down wages.

Also, if your woman has girlfriends with problems that can be clearly explained from a red pilled perspective, be sure to point them out. Perhaps a few of her friends are single mothers. This can be a way you can showcase how such life choices have a negative impact on women's lives, and you want better for her.

-What habits and decisions have most helped your platform to grow?

I have always valued quality over quantity. There are people who produce a vast amount of content at a low visual or audio level, but generally what they have to say gains interest. I make sure that my content is well thought out. I often write a script, fact check my points, and spend multiple days thinking it over before filming. I try to use the best audio and video recording that I can afford at this time, and that also helped me gain subscribers

In the beginning many complained about my audio. When I bought a better microphone, those complaints disappeared and people were more willing to subscribe.

I also focus on what interests people. By this, I mean that I focus on current news cycles and subjects that impact people day to day. When I keep up with current trends, current news cycles, and current talking points, I tend to gain more interest. But it also has to be a topic that interests me. Otherwise I can't maintain a certain level of productivity for an extended period of time.

-What are we fighting for in the culture war and why does this matter?

I have always seen the culture war as a fight for the preservation of the best qualities my people possess. Traits that white men are known for such as the need to explore, go farther, and create a better world for our progeny. We give more to the world than we take. We build highway systems, space rockets, music, literature, etc.

In order to build and create beyond ourselves, we must have a functioning society that respects men. White men have been intentionally targeted as the root of evil in modern society and white women have been taught to turn against them. Yet the more we see whites flee various cities or areas, the more we see degeneracy and crime. My fight to preserve my people is an effort to see goodness prevail. If we dwindle into a global minority more so than we already are and we allow ourselves to be shamed for the color of our skin, I believe we will see a dark time where mankind as a whole takes giant steps backward. And given that I want a better world for my children, not a worse one, I dedicate a certain number of hours every week to fighting in the culture war.

FIGHT

Who We Are Fighting Against

The basic ideas we are fighting against are:

-that government has the solutions to complex social problems

-that we are all equal and thus no borders should exist between us

-that everyone should submit to Allah or die

-that America should be the world's policeman in service of hostile foreign interests

These ideas are mentioned again, under their proper ideological umbrellas in the "Globalists" section soon to follow, but they bear mentioning at the outset of this essay. The elite have long known that their fight is less against ideas, though ideas are potent and can change the world, but against the people who hold the ideas. An assassination here, a beheading there, and voilà! the problem has been resolved for the time being. They have managed things this way for centuries.

With the Internet, we are able to identify who the bad actors are in society. From there, we work to defeat them with arguments and to socially ostracize them. If enough people are convinced of their treachery, voting patterns will change and a political solution will be achieved. The elite fear this more than anything in the world. It's a clean victory. They have always won the dirty battles but if their power is undermined sufficiently, they don't have a leg to stand on in the public eye.

What follows is a list of the major players who are destroying the liberties that were bought with blood in the West.

The International Power Elite

Prominent members of the international power elite include the Bush Dynasty, the Clintons, leaders of major European states including Angela Merkel and Emanuel Macron, elements of the Saudi Royal Family, Oprah, Leonardo DiCaprio, Mark Zuckerberg, Bill Gates, Richard Branson, Jeff Bezos, Carlos Slim, Michael Bloomberg, Jeffrey Epstein, Larry Page, and Canadian PM Justin Trudeau.

Noteworthy corporations in the international power elite include State Street Corporation, Rothschild & Co, and Goldman Sachs Group.

The international power elite is basically defined as super wealthy or super powerful people or corporations who advance the aims of one world government through multiculturalism, technocracy, and equality.

Not all super wealthy or super powerful people are Communist douchebags, for example: Donald Trump, Jack Ma, and Peter Thiel. The list of decent to good guys is short, however.

The international power elite utilizes the mainstream media[48] to flood Muslims, Mexicans, and Africans into the West. They use the World Bank[49] to take over countries that threaten to break away from the central banking hegemony that primarily enriches the Rothschild banking clan. They use their wealth to fund studies[50], NGOs, and lobbying that undermines national sovereignty.

Through what has traditionally been termed "The Mob", the international power elite floods the West with opiates and psychedelics to break the brains of the young and erode the will of the morally courageous. These super elite preach for open borders from behind gated compounds and grizzled mercenary bodyguards[51].

---

[48]Jeff Bezos owns the Washington Post. Carlos Slim owns the New York Times.
[49]http://www.imdb.com/title/tt4172710/?ref_=fn_al_tt_1
[50]http://www.gatesfoundation.org/
[51]http://www.breitbart.com/big-hollywood/2017/05/23/katie-perry-on-manchester-bombing-no-barriers-no-borders-we-all-

Since time immemorial, the wealthy have been able to compensate for their crimes with boatloads of cash. People all too often have a price point where their conscience is bought out. Direct cultural attacks on the power elite will not yield game changing results until their rampaging hydra, the mainstream media, is undone.

The Mainstream Media

The worse propagandists of the mainstream media are CIA psyops more than they are anything related to true news: CNN, the Washington Post, the NY Times, BBC, Huffington Post, CBC, MSNBC, CBS, ABC, NBC, and most major city newspapers. These companies often employ former CIA interns[52] and the sons and daughters of Washington DC plutocrats to craft narratives that serve the interests of the world's power elite. The trespasses of the mainstream media are too numerous[53] [54] [55] to catalogue here but they have certainly earned the moniker "Fake News".

---

just-need-to-co-exist/

[52]http://mentalfloss.com/article/87129/11-things-you-might-not-know-about-anderson-cooper

[53]https://twitter.com/Cernovich/status/871490252765921280

[54]http://www.breitbart.com/big-government/2017/01/14/fake-news-wash-post-changes-story-on-trump-firing-d-c-natl-guard-general/

[55]http://www.breitbart.com/big-journalism/2017/06/04/fake-news-nbc-correction-after-claiming-putin-had-compromising-info-

The mainstream media has also lost the trust of the American people, according to a Gallup poll[56] in early 2017 that has revealed a steady decline in trust for the past 20 years.

The mainstream media is particularly dangerous because it has the power to convince common Americans to support such atrocities as the War on Drugs, the liberal war on the family institution, the cults of diversity and multiculturalism, and endless foreign military intervention. This is achieved through the staging of false events, manipulation through appeals to sentimentalism and emotion, and the spreading of false or highly questionable intelligence reports[57]. Public schooling sets people up by removing their ability to think independently and the mainstream media knocks them down with award winning propaganda.

Too long has the media poisoned the minds of the American people. Fortunately, independent journalists, platformers, and speakers are knocking the hell out of the media. People are ending their cable TV subscriptions at an ever-increasing rate[58] and homeschooling is trending upwards at a staggering pace[59].

---

trump/
[56]http://wjla.com/news/nation-world/main-stream-media-continue-to-lose-the-publics-trust
[57]https://www.rt.com/news/378695-oscar-white-helmets-win/

The mainstream media is the largest and most important domino to fall. It is the sick glue that binds together and consolidates the power of the groups undermining the West. To paraphrase Alex Jones, "We are in an information war for the soul of mankind."

It may be interesting to dig into questions of the doctrine, philosophy, and future of the conservative movement, but we need to keep our eyes on the prize: destroy all credibility of the corporate media and set the minds of Westerners free. Infighting does not matter. The passport system for a moon base of 130+ IQ only people does not matter. What matters in this democratic West we live in is that the stranglehold on people's minds is broken. Otherwise, people will continue to vote for and support all the sick assaults and affronts to the very existence of Western Civilization. When CNN is bankrupt and off the air, we can get into the small differences between us.

Political Islam

Islam, which means "submission", is a monotheistic death cult invented by a pedophile goat-herder warlord in the Middle East around the 7th century. Muslims are adherents of Islam. In 2015 they

---

[58]http://fortune.com/2016/04/05/household-cable-cord-cutters/
[59]http://www.cnsnews.com/news/article/terence-p-jeffrey/1773000-homeschooled-children-618-10-years

were 24.1% of the world's population[60]. Islam is the fastest growing "religion" in the world and are expected to comprise 31.1% of the world's population by 2060.

Islam masquerades as a religion but it is in fact a political, world dominating ideology. There is nothing benign or benevolent about its teachings though every now and then an adherent can do something kind for someone else (and promptly be lionized by the media). The aim of Islam is to totally saturate the globe with Sharia law and to convert or kill all non-believers through jihad, holy war. As Islam expert Bill Warner says, "Islam is the most successful totalitarian system in history. There are post-Communist societies and post-Nazi societies but, there are no post Islamic societies."[61]

There can exist no friendship or good will with someone who is ideologically opposed to your continued existence as a non-adherent of Islam. Anyone who acts as a friend to Islam is either an absolute traitor to the West or is involved in some political subterfuge to try and gain ground for the West. There is no neutrality in the face of a world-dominating ideology. The Muslims have known this for centuries and have acted accordingly. Those in the West are only just

---

[60]http://www.pewresearch.org/fact-tank/2017/04/06/why-muslims-are-the-worlds-fastest-growing-religious-group/
[61]https://www.politicalislam.com/political-islam-totalitarian-doctrine/

waking up to the unending menace of Abrahamic submission.

Islam is foreign to the West. It is not of the West. It was spawned in the Middle East. It is alien. It has no place in the West.

Perspectives: Pamela Geller

twitter.com/pamelageller

Pamela Geller is the editor and publisher of the Geller Report and author of *FATWA: Hunted in America*[62], a popular book chronicling the battle to defeat the sinister Ground Zero mosque project and an Islamic assassination order placed on Ms.Geller.

-What strategies and habits have contributed to your media reach the most?

I tell truths that the establishment media and even many conservatives want to conceal or fear to tell. There are always people who appreciate the truth being fully told, and it's a rare thing these days.

-What are two aspects of Islam most regular Americans aren't aware of?

Its doctrines of violence, misogyny and anti-Semitism are not twistings of Islam, but are embedded in the Quran. And

---

[62]http://a.co/5O6pWxT

government and law enforcement have been deeply
compromised by Muslim Brotherhood operatives.

-What do young people need to know the most in order to
contribute to the West?

They need to know the value of our Western culture and
civilization. This will make them determined to defend the
West.

Perspectives: Julian Langness pt. 2
twitter.com/J_Langness

Julian is the author of *Fistfights With Muslims In*
Europe: One Man's Journey Through Modernity. It is a book
about his travels in Europe over a five-year span in the 2000's
and how they impacted his personal and political journey.

Given this background, I wanted to include some of
Julian's thoughts on Islam in this section of the book.

What do people need to know about Islam in Europe?

They need to know that, over the last half-century,
European leaders have flooded the Western and Southern
portions of the continent with Muslim immigrants who now
make up a very sizeable percentage of the overall population,
and a dangerously sizable percentage of the under 35 year old

demographic within that population. The reasons this has taken place are enormously complicated.

In part it was the naivety of a generation of leaders born into the greatest prosperity in world history, who were blind to the realities of existence.

In part it was due to their focus on short-term emotional satisfaction rather than long-term responsibility.

In part it was due to utopianism and their belief that they were creating "the just, fair, multicultural society of the future".

In part it was due to the machinations of wealthy globalist elites.

And in part it was due to simple human inertia, and the intractable flow of globalization.

Today, according to various analysts, Germany either has or will by 2020 have a non-European majority among 18-35 year old men. Sweden has the second highest per capita rape rate on earth after Johannesburg, South Africa. Native Europeans are not having enough children to replace themselves yet the Muslim immigrant population has above replacement rate fertility and would be growing even without continued migration taking place.

As a result of all this- if nothing changes and Europe continues upon its current trajectory- nations such as France, Belgium, the Netherlands, Germany, the UK, and Sweden will absolutely end up being majority Muslim countries. Some nations might still be able to avert this through the proper political developments, yet we have seen few victories for political parties wishing to avoid such a fate. It is possible that no political efforts will be made toward halting this eventuality and that the nations of Western Europe will eventually fall into anarchy and violence and/or full Islamization.

These facts are largely ignored in the international press, but what is happening in Europe today is the most significant development in the three-thousand year recorded history of European culture.

Events today might lack the bloodshed of various wars from Europe's past, but the long-term demographic results will far exceed WWI, WWII, the Mongol Invasions, or even the Bubonic Plague. It is tempting to think that some government or leader will arrive to save the day, but I'm afraid it is up to us, collectively and individually, to prevent such an outcome from occurring.

In my opinion, it will be the sum total of our individual efforts that will determine what comes to pass. Normally, I think the most important question for a man should be "How can I become the best man I can be?" However, today, I think the question of "How best can I contribute to the fight to save Western civilization" is equally important.

Because really, they are the same question.

Baby Boomers

Baby Boomers are Americans who were born in 1946 to 1964, roughly speaking. From Wikipedia[63]:

> Baby boomers were the wealthiest, most active, and most physically fit generation up to the era in which they arrived, and were amongst the first to grow up genuinely expecting the world to improve with time. They were also the generation that received peak levels of income; they could therefore reap the benefits of abundant levels of food, apparel, retirement programs, and sometimes even "midlife crisis" products. The increased consumerism for this generation has been regularly criticized as excessive.

Baby Boomers got swept up in the countercultural revolution of the 1960's, brought on partly by the advent of cheap birth control and partly by globalist subterfuge through academia[64]. Their formative brain development years were shaped by bored suburban mothers after a war effort and by drugs and easy sex in early adulthood. Boomers went on to

---

[63]https://en.wikipedia.org/wiki/Baby_boomers
[64]http://mailstar.net/macdonald.html

previously unimaginable financial heights. With a dollar unpegged from the gold standard[65] and a government exploding in size[66], Baby Boomers went on to massively reshape the United States into a consumerist dystopia. Credit cards essentially grew on trees and McMansions sprouted up from the freshly tilled soil. TV dinners and abortions skyrocketed, as well.

The Baby Boomers, stupefied by television, failed to value the moral courage and commitment to civic and religious traditions that made America great in the first place. They lost their way and voted for Bush instead of Buchanan, Clinton instead of Perot, and McCain/Obama instead of Ron Paul. Boomers failed to stem the Mexican flood pouring into the country, choosing instead to buy "one more cute SUV for mother once the children left the nest". They failed to police the inner cities in America, falling prey to the newspeak term "racist". They worshipped their sports idols while American manufacturing died at the hands of NAFTA. They traded in their farmers for air conditioners.

The gravy train of easy credit, McMansions, consequence-free sex, and "get a job in the tech industry

---

[65]https://www.federalreservehistory.org/essays/gold_convertibility _ends
[66]https://en.wikipedia.org/wiki/Great_Society

or government" is coming to an end. The children of the Boomers and their children's children will inherit the mess the older generation is partly ducking out on. The white flight is running out. There's nowhere to run to because everything is turning into a ghetto overseen by corporations and police state thugs.

Baby Boomers continue to stand in the way, particularly and especially in Europe where French voters for Rothschild stoolie Emanuel Macron averaged an age of 65 compared to 35 for the courageous but defeated Marine Le Pen[67]. To their credit, many Boomers voted for Trump over Clinton[68].

There is some hope for Boomers to lean their financial weight away from the corporations, banks, and governmental agencies that seek to rule their children and grandchildren. Boomers are now dying out and we'll see how many we can bring over to our side against the Left. The age of the "cuckservative[69]" is ending. Some of them, like Newt Gingrich[70] and Rush

[67]http://www.breitbart.com/london/2017/05/08/macron-younger-average-voter-youth-flocked-le-pen/
[68]http://www.pewresearch.org/fact-tank/2016/11/09/behind-trumps-victory-divisions-by-race-gender-education/
[69]http://a.co/3coxphG
[70]http://www.salon.com/2017/03/13/the-potomac-purge-newt-gingrich-supports-donald-trumps-plan-to-drastically-downsize-federal-government/

Limbaugh[71], have seen the sea change and are jumping on board.

Baby Boomers are in no way outsiders to the West. They are not part of the out-group. They are our parents, grandparents, and elders. The approach we ought to take with them is much less contentious than the groups previously mentioned. It is much easier to convert a Boomer than a CIA stooge working for NBC. There are good things about the Boomer generation, particularly their conscientiousness. It's time their conscientiousness is not used against them anymore. Boomers, who want it, need their shot at redemption.

Globalists

Globalists undermine the cultural, social, and legal sovereignty of the peoples of the West. Globalism is marked by the following movements, groups, or talking points:

-foreign secret service operations within the United States

-foreign lobbying in Washington D.C.

-Hollywood

---

[71]http://www.breitbart.com/video/2016/12/05/rush-limbaugh-offense-donald-trump/

-open borders

-multiculturalism

-free trade deals that undermine the West

-international finance (Rothschilds, Soros, Goldman Sachs)

-the Federal Reserve

-neoconservatism

-cosmopolitanism

-circumcision

-the United Nations, WHO, and World Bank

-the Frankfurt School

-psychoanalysis and sexual "liberation"

-the professional victim industry

-the professional protestor industry

-the humanities in academia

-multiculturalism

-political correctness

-Communism

Globalists act as an out-group when they engage in win-lose psychoevolutionary strategies against the original peoples of the West. Globalism best thrives in circumstances of ethnic pluralism, where minority groups with strong in-group identities can operate under the radar. The ethnic peoples of the West best thrive in ethnocentric, nationalistic societies. There has been a concerted and conscious effort on the part of countless globalists to undermine the West. It is particularly worth highlighting Barack Obama, Sigmund Freud, George Soros, Franz Boas, Woody Allen, Hillary Clinton, John Lennon, Steven Spielberg, David Geffen, the Council on Foreign Relations, Winston Churchill, Sumner Redstone Rothstein, and Ted Turner.

Globalists fear two things the most: being labeled as globalists and experiencing systemic hostility for their globalist status. This book is only very partially concerned with the first and I do not advocate for the second.

What this book does advocate for is to learn from the in-group strategies of the most powerful in-groups in the world: the international elite, the globalists (often one and the same), and political Islamists.

Name the first eight famous people you can think of. At least one or two of them will be globalists or subjugates and supporters of the aims of globalist world hegemony.

One note on the culture war worth mentioning is that once it was apparent Donald J. Trump would be the Republican candidate in the 2016 election, Reddit's "the Donald forum" was promptly taken over by politically correct administrators who banned all mentions of race realism as "scientific racism". These people were then quick to promote soft globalist interests in the top posts of the forum where it had previously been a largely true Western, grassroots affair. This is the power of the globalists.

Globalists are in charge of all the major tech companies based out of Silicon Valley. They enforce the norms of political correctness, multiculturalism, international finance, and large multinational governing bodies at the expense of people's free thought.

Getting Into The Culture War: Punching At Your Weight

The right wing, free speech side of the culture war needs all the help it can get right now. The list of prominent right-wingers with a sizeable platform is not all that extensive:

-Donald Trump

-Alex Jones

-Ann Coulter

-Tucker Carlson

-Paul Joseph Watson

-Stefan Molyneux

-Sean Hannity

-Lauren Southern

-Mike Cernovich

-Ron Paul

-Rand Paul

-Steven Crowder

-Donald Trump Jr.

-Mark Dice

-Tommy Robinson

Toss in maybe another 40 or 50 and you've got the full list. That's out of approximately 1.1 billion people living in the USA, Europe, Canada, Australia, and New Zealand.

We need more culture warriors who will stand for free speech and pro-civilizational values. This will be the difference maker in our mission to defeat globalism and save the West.

The great thing about a market demand is that people will flock to fill it. I encourage everyone who wants to join in the battle to save civilization to go on ahead and jump on in.

Media platforms are built by gradually accumulated credibility in the free market of ideas. Lots of young people wanting to make a difference for society *right this second* skip over this basic fact and try punch way above their weight. They don't look for allies and opponents in their own weight class and relegate themselves to retweeting people they may never have personal access to. However, even this is better than sitting on the sidelines.

I mention punching at your weight because I have found it is the best way to up your power levels in the culture war. I try to tackle the meta-political ideas, strategies, and challenges that lie directly before me on my path to helping the world become a freer place. Donald Trump has bigger fish to fry. I get it. But I have fish to fry, too. And when I'm done frying those fish, I can fry bigger and bigger fish!

By committing oneself to a sober analysis of what lies before them on the path to building a platform, a person gives themselves the best chance to grow steadily and consistently rather than in fits and spurts. Fits and spurts are good, too, however. Whatever it takes. Consistency and persistence are the key advantages we have over the liberals and leftists threatening to ruin the West forever. They are the ones who more often get sudden platforms because of cushy, once a week, columns that serve corporate interests.

We all have to start somewhere. Your first YouTube video likely won't be a smashing success that will catapult you to major relevance in the fight to save civilization... unless you come from a noteworthy background of competence and consistency in some other field. Tim Allen could start a Dave Rubin style web show and have instant, major success. Good for him! We could use him!

But most of us will start at the bottom with little relevance and little useful feedback. When we punch at our own weight, we get involved with people with larger platforms than us and provide them value however reasonably they ask for it.

Someone asking for book sales? Jump in and then let people know how the book was!

Someone asking for donations? Fork it over.

Someone asking us to trend a hashtag? Get on that, young warrior.

Over time our power levels grow. We become people of reputation. We become able to lend a hand to those who come after us. There is enough room at the table! No need to bring others down to bring oneself up. We have all got to be of use to each other.

And who knows? Every now and then one of us will bust loose to supernova into the cultural conversation. You won't know until you try.

Saul Alinksy's Rules for Radicals

"A racially integrated community is a chronological term timed from the entrance of the first black family to the exit of the last white family."

-Saul Alinsky

Divided into ten chapters, *Rules for Radicals*[72] provides lessons on how a community organizer can accomplish the goal of successfully uniting people into an active organization with the power to effect change on a variety of issues. Though targeted at community organization, these chapters also touch on other issues that range from ethics, education, communication, and symbol construction to nonviolence and political philosophy.

Alinksy's goal for the *Rules for Radicals* was to create a guide for future community organizers to use in uniting low-income communities, or "Have-Nots", in order for them to gain social, political, legal, and economic power over ethnic Europeans.

Rules for Radicals is a handbook for activists to bring about Communism in the United States. Alinksy's most prominent students have been Barack Hussein Obama and Hillary Clinton. His ideas, outlined in a moment, have come to dominate political discourse in the United States, gaining implementation primarily through the mainstream media.

This is an overview of his ideas and what we on the side of freedom can do about them. If we are going to be effective in the culture war, we have to come to

---

[72]https://en.wikipedia.org/wiki/Rules_for_Radicals

terms with the playbook that has been guiding cultural Marxists since the early 1970's.

The Rules:

1. *"Power is not only what you have, but what the enemy thinks you have." Power is derived from two main sources – money and people. "Have-Nots" must build power from flesh and blood.*

The right wing has been fighting back, for the first time ever, by crowd funding the legal defense of people who have been targeted by the Left. The Right has also started to show up in force to protests staged by the Left. The Right generally does not benefit from international finance but it is starting to learn to make up for it with boots on the ground. Leftists are now being confronted by their opposition and they are getting nice and triggered over it.

2. *"Never go outside the expertise of your people." It results in confusion, fear and retreat. Feeling secure adds to the backbone of anyone.*

There is a deliberate avoidance on the part of leftists toward straying into areas in which they have no real knowledge. The Right is now turning this rule and the next one around on the Left by engaging leftists with questions such as, "Can you define fascism for me?" or by getting them to sign petitions against their own stated interests. The Right is learning that in the face of the enemy you need not engage in speculation or open-ended dialogue, you simply attack the areas of weakness the Left has. You do this over and over, mercilessly.

3. *"Whenever possible, go outside the expertise of the enemy." Look for ways to increase insecurity, anxiety and uncertainty.*

See above.

4. *"Make the enemy live up to its own book of rules." If the rule is that every letter gets a reply, send 30,000 letters. You can kill them with this because no one can possibly obey all of their own rules.*

We live in an age where people have decided to declare themselves "trans-black"[73], "attack helicopters", and "non-gendered." The absurdity of all this is becoming clear. Fathers are fighting back against feminism by holding feminists to the same standards they have been held to. Organizations such as Turning Point USA and activists in the West have begun cloaking themselves in identity politics as a means of short-circuiting the rules the Left has been operating by.

---

[73]http://wjla.com/news/offbeat/rachel-dolezal-says-she-identifies-as-trans-black

5. "Ridicule is man's most potent weapon." There is no defense. It's irrational. It's infuriating. It also works as a key pressure point to force the enemy into concessions.

Meme warfare, at its best, is pure ridicule. For too long have the imps gotten away with biting and biting at the sleeping giant. The giant has woken up and is pinning these imps to the wall, to watch them squirm. There is no moral strength in the Left. As such, they are easy prey now. It is easy to point out the perversion of nearly naked "men" dancing in gay pride parades alongside little boys. It is easy to hint at people being pedophiles by implying they like "pizza". Twitter is filled with vicious negs of leftists trying to engage in victimhood politics.

Ridicule works. Donald Trump himself blew this open for the Right by calling Marco Rubio "little" and saying Jeb Bush was "low energy". Ridicule that is true sticks forever.

6. "A good tactic is one your people enjoy." They'll keep doing it without urging and come back to do more. They're doing their thing, and will even suggest better ones.

This is a prelude to meme warfare itself. Tactics have to be catchy. Right now it is infectious to go to left wing protests and agitate them with better arguments and insults. Nobody with any substance on the right has to be cajoled into going and doing this. You can simply offer a car ride over and make good sport out of it. The same goes for retweeting prominent leftists with your spiciest digs attached. It's just good ole' fun! Everyone gets to have a laugh when Trump sticks it again and again to Rosie O'Donnell or his political opponents in the intelligence agencies.

7. *"A tactic that drags on too long becomes a drag." Don't become old news.*

The Left has used "cry baby" tactics for too long and it is old as sin now. Cry-bullying is old news. It's not a good look. Most everyone on the right is waking up to this. Leftist Baby Boomers cry-bullied their way into massive pensions and Ponzi schemes to defraud future generations. The future generations are onto this. They are learning that, because of historically lean economic activity, you have to work hard and be honest to get what you want in this life. Besides, posting a video to YouTube of someone cry-bullying you is instant viral video status. Piling on cry-bullies is becoming an American way of life!

Another tactic the Left has used for too long has been to call people "racist". During the Baby Boomer generation, this label was a surefire way to disable people making sound arguments for freedom or simply expressing their preference not to be overrun by the Third World. The term "racist" is so played out now that it has no real meaning, no real damaging power.

8. *"Keep the pressure on. Never let up." Keep trying new things to keep the opposition off balance. As the opposition masters one approach, hit them from the flank with something new.*

The wrecking of the US economy and social fabric has left a lot of angry, young men without steady, full-time jobs. As such, they have plenty of time to battle the Left on the Internet. They devote themselves to this with fervor. It's like real-life video games. There are few worse stabs to the heart than being dispossessed of the society your forefathers endeavored. These young men won't be forgetting the way they were vilified in academia and public schools. Nor will their children. The Left can count on being harangued relentlessly. It will never end for the Left, from here on out. The freedom movement memed a President into the White House. This is a lesson not soon forgotten!

9. *"The threat is usually more terrifying than the thing itself." Imagination and ego can dream up many more consequences than any activist.*

Leftists are terrified of "fascism", though most of them cannot define it. Simply show them pictures of straight white males bonding and they will shriek with hysterical fear. The specter of Western male cohesion is terrifying to all the traitors and invaders of the West because they fear collective punishment for what they have done. Nobody actually knows if that day will ever come or if things will even be qualified in that manner. But the boogeyman lurks.

10. *"The major premise for tactics is the development of operations that will maintain a constant pressure upon the opposition." It is this unceasing pressure that results in the reactions from the opposition that are essential for the success of the campaign.*

Communist technocrats like Bill Gates and Mark Zuckerberg, who pose as "green capitalists", allowed us the means of instant shitposting thanks to their contributions to technology. While Google higher-ups sit in their lavish offices glad handing with CIA operatives at all the control they think they have, they do not realize their weapons can be turned against them. Their precious positions rely on the enforcement of intellectual property laws that can easily be circumvented through simple disregard, some encryption, and a few anti-trust federal lawsuits.

Technology is morally neutral but its wielders and advocates can be outsmarted and outfoxed, always.

11. *"If you push a negative hard enough, it will push through and become a positive."* Violence from the other side can win the public to your side because the public sympathizes with the underdog.

With the ever-increasing social footprint of black conservatism, the cultural narrative is starting to shift away from the iconic images burned into everyone's minds of blacks holding sit-ins in the 1960's. The mainstream media no longer has the stranglehold on the American they once had through the television networks. Cable is losing hundreds of thousands of subscribers every month. They will never gain those subscribers back. A more accurate documentation is emerging of how the Democrats have mobilized people to act against their own interests.

12. *"The price of a successful attack is a constructive alternative."* Never let the enemy score points because you're caught without a solution to the problem.

The Right must be willing to set the tone and agenda for any compromises that are arranged with the Left. The Left has known this for decades upon decades. They agitate and attack and gain ground all the while.

The Right is *just* beginning to understand this. You *must* take the fight to the Left and take their ground away from them. There is no sense in pondering solutions if the other side doesn't care about solutions. You simply push for territory and let the chips lie where they will after the fact. There is no gentlemanly decorum here to observe because you cannot hold higher standards than those who seek your destruction. There is no real negotiation anymore, only compromise based on where the power lies.

The globalist left has long churned out fake conservatives, placed in positions in the media to then offer up "compromises" with the Left. We are now seeing conservatives don the garb of the liberal left and offer up olive branches in the other direction.

13. *"Pick the target, freeze it, personalize it, and polarize it." Cut off the support network and isolate the target from sympathy. Go after people and not institutions; people hurt faster than institutions.*

Many people on 4chan, Reddit, and Twitter have been saying things like, "John Podesta is a dead man walking". The former Clinton campaign manager and White House Chief of Staff has been implicated in crimes of the most heinous nature. The court of public opinion is set against him and he is openly being called a pedophile by right wingers with no backlash. Even a

Rothschild, Lynn de Rothschild, has disavowed Podesta by tweeting, "this is pathetic, HRC lost because you ran an arrogant out of touch campaign, you have destroyed a great family and are a loser" on Feb. 21st, 2017. Podesta has lost the support of the wealthiest family in the history of mankind.

We will see who he outs and takes down with him and if the proverbial swamp will ever be drained. He's frozen, isolated, and polarized. Andrew Breitbart may yet be avenged.

John Podesta is one of the first to be targeted, frozen, personalized, and polarized but he will not be the last. James Comey, former director of the FBI, is another person that has faced ostracism and ridicule for his evil deeds. The Right can now do to alleged Deep State pedophiles what the Left once did to Kenneth Starr.

Saul Alinsky was part of the Frankfurt School of social theory. These were a group of globalist cranks who loathed the freedoms and standard of living in the United States. They did everything in their intellectual power to deconstruct what made America so great. They sought to break down ethnic and national barriers so that Communism could gain a strong foothold in

North America. They succeeded to a large degree. We are now attempting to right their wrongs and usher in a new era of freedom.

Rules for Radicals is a weapon that can be turned on its master, and easily so.

Those working in the free market have always had the better arguments. Now they possess the superior tactics that have been plied against them for so long. Let's all enjoy as they proceed to mop up leftists in the realm of public discourse and political power. Hopefully it will be enough before the absolute math of demographics kicks into full gear.

Put Up or Shut Up

We live in an age of major bad-mouthing. If you're a content creator you have probably experienced sniping from people with anonymous accounts on whatever social media platform you're on. They shoot little, petty nitpicking comments your way. They try to psychologize you. Some of them will do whatever it takes to get under your skin.

What's the common theme?

Most of the time they are not content creators themselves. You put yourself out on the line to try to make a difference in the world with your creativity and originality. They come in and try to crap on you. Why?

They are envious and insecure. They are not creative or original themselves. As such, they have no idea what a struggle it can be to remain persistent and consistent with manifesting truth in the world. They are lazy. They are pathetic.

They want you to feel what they feel so you will be miserable in their company.

Some of them even create content but they do it at a very low level, like robots spitting out re-interpretations of things that have already been said and less effectively so. These are the most envious of them all. They know they don't have that next-level gear so they try to deny your own brilliance. They're average. They masquerade as great, but they are so pathetically average and boring.

Results matter. If you are busy working to save civilization and seeing results, you have no time for unoriginal or altogether uncreative wankers with little to no influence.

Written a book on a subject? See how it sells, how it is praised or critiqued, and then understand that someone who has not gone through this reflective process on a work of their own is in no position to criticize you. They have not gone where you have gone.

Someone who read the Wikipedia on an event that you have released several videos on to thousands of people, garnering lots of feedback, may think they're on equal footing with respect to influence but most of the time they're not. They have to put up, by making videos of their own, or shut up.

Little is ever actually accomplished anymore on message boards and comments sections on videos. The most elite content creators will, at most, respond to comments with a few words or maybe a short video. There are bigger fish to fry. Take issue with something a content creator said? Create your own content rebutting it and let the marketplace decide whose ideas are more relevant and actionable. If content creators stooped to thoroughly responding to a person's every bitchy comment on YouTube, they wouldn't get anything done. That's not the name of the game. The name of the game is put up or shut up.

Once you start trying to add value to the lives of others by creating actionable, provocative, and enriching content, you will start to see content creators less as unjust parents to snipe at and more as other people, trying to make a difference. The only way to

190

grow a platform is to make relevant content. In order to know what's relevant and plug away at it, you have to have some semblance of empathy. You start to figure out that approaching people collaboratively, in the spirit of creativity, will serve you much better than spoiling for a fight wherever you go.

Let's face it: it takes courage to look into a camera and speak to the public about your ideas on things, particularly in the countries with no free speech assurances. You have to be well-reasoned, have order and structure to your thoughts, try to be likeable, and come up with new ideas. It takes courage. Courage is out in the open. Cowardice hides behind veils. All of us who create things in the free market are hoping you'll put up rather than shut up. We need your help.

Perspectives: Tara McCarthy
twitter.com/TaraMcCarthy444

Tara McCarthy is a popular YouTuber and platformer known for her many interviews with leading experts dealing with intelligence, demographics, and the culture war.

-What habits, strategies, and values have contributed to you building up your social media platform?

The reason my social media platforms have grown is because I'm obsessed about talking about the topics that I talk about. I can't not talk about them. If that's you, you're probably already posting about this kind of stuff on your 'normie' social media profiles in a muted fashion, and either being ignored or criticized for doing so.

You need to open new social media profiles where you feel comfortable going all out. And just stick with those profiles creating high quality content as often as you can without burning out. Eventually you will attract people who think the same way as you. I also recommend that once you have a decent amount of content up that you contact some others who are more established than you are and ask if you can interview them or vice versa.

I don't recommend bothering with Facebook at this stage. At this point in time, you'll get far more reach on YouTube and Twitter – but if you only pick one, YouTube is the best because you can convey more complex ideas and, this sounds weird but you bond with your audience better when they can see and hear you. Podcasts are also a great option.

There's no need to use your real name to begin with, but expect to be doxxed (have someone maliciously reveal your full name, address etc. on the internet or newspapers). SJWs Always Lie *by Vox Day is a great book to read to accustom you to the types of attacks that you will receive. So, You've Been Publicly Shamed *by Jon Ronson is another book that I recommend you read before you start so that you know what you're getting yourself into.*

You must be willing to take hits, and to say goodbye to a normal life. And to do this you must absolutely believe that what you're doing is the right thing to do, and that it's bigger than you and even your family.

-Why is the West worth the effort?

Look around the world and ask yourself what kind of countries you'd like your great grandchildren to live in. Chances are the third world hell holes that many of today's migrants are coming from are not the places you pick. As we've seen, migrants tend to bring their cultures, their IQs, their work ethic, and their criminality with them when they move.

If you like living in a high IQ, peaceful, high trust, functioning society – that's Western Civilization, and it will cease to exist if we don't protect it.

-How can more women get into the culture war?

Although I was previously highly skeptical about what could be achieved through voting, after seeing Trump's election in 2016, and Brexit in the UK, I have been convinced that influencing elections is in fact a very powerful way to help us achieve our goals of halting and reversing the current demographic trends.

Since women are half of the voting population, it makes sense that we seek to appeal to them, and we can do this by speaking with them about how mass immigration negatively affects their own lives by way of housing prices, children's schooling, safety for women on the streets etc. We can also seek to create nationalist spaces online and in the real world that women will enjoy being part of.

Most women are not going to be willing to take the very real risks associated with speaking publicly about the problems with immigration and multiculturalism in the West. However, as the ideas become more mainstream and thus less dangerous to hold, more women will feel able to publicly identify with them.

So overall, we should be seeking to appeal to the general population. Both men and women.

The Smallness of Leftism

The main characteristic of a person who cannot perceive their own redundancy and obsolescence is smallness. This is one of the primary symptoms of leftism. The best example of smallness embodied is Hillary Clinton. She chose to drag the Democratic Party through the meat grinder of her personal lack of touch with reality to the point where it is in institutional ruins. For better or worse, she's been the leader of all leftists in the United States.

Here are the issues she ran on in 2016:

-Raise taxes on the middle class.

This is redundant and antiquated because the middle class has been paying the lion's share of taxes in the United States for generations now. The middle class is sick of being leached on and told they are insensitive racists when they are the primary wealth creators in our economy. They are tired of seeing their status shrink as untold billions of dollars have gone overseas to China. The middle class is sick of being set against the wealthy and seeing the opportunities to join the wealthy shrink as a result.

-We must continue to expand opportunities for Americans with disabilities.

Hillary shows little understanding that people are onto her "level the playing field" ploys, using the disabled members of society as mascots for expanded welfare programs. A society with more moral courage, as is starting to emerge, would be a society where those with disabilities would find employment and private health insurance at affordable rates. Disability rights is just one more "battle for smallness" that people are sick of seeing their hard earned money stolen to pay for. The disabled in our country have more rights, more wealth, and more consideration than in any other country in the world. It's time to stop loading government ineptitude onto them.

-Lesbian, gay, bisexual, and transgender Americans deserve to live their lives free from discrimination.

These kinds of people are a small percentage of the population. The Left is all too eager to parade these people around like mascots and offer them every government program in the world. Hillary Clinton and her ilk have a cynical view on LGBT people, just like they do on the disabled. These are undignified "snowflakes" on which to dump every government program available. LGBTs have had fantastic treatment in the West and everyone is sick of holding their tongues about how the Left uses them as political pawns.

-America's long struggle with race is far from finished.

Whites are made culpable for slavery in all the public school curriculums when only 2-3% of them in the South owned slaves. Meanwhile, Jews owned 25-40%[74]. Whites have been made the perpetual boogeyman for every non-white failure and crime in the United States; Yet non-whites have been treated far better in the United States than anywhere else throughout history. The contrast between how minorities do in the USA versus back in their home countries is staggering, almost without exception.

---

[74]http://history.stackexchange.com/questions/17711/   ish-slave-owners-in-the-united-states

Hillary is right in that her side, the liberals, want to kick off a new era of racial struggles by flooding Muslims into an already multicultural situation with whites and blacks watching their jobs get stolen by illegal aliens. Her campaign issue here of, "America's long struggle with race is far from finished" sounds more like a veiled threat, given we know that her husband wanted to "rebuild Detroit" with Somalians[75].

-Addiction and substance use: Through improved treatment, prevention, and training, we can end this quiet epidemic once and for all.

When it comes to drugs, those on the Left are quick to point out the "successes" of Vancouver, British Columbia, to justify their massive government spending on addicts. "See, they can shoot up heroin in a safe place! We need more clinics like this and then everyone is safe." Treating drug users with compassion is understandable and can pull people out of deep holes, but that's beside the point. What leftists fail to recognize is that drugs destroy people's sense of boundaries and thus their recognition of in-groups and out-groups.

---

[75]http://www.breitbart.com/2016-presidential-race/2016/08/29/bill-clinton-calls-for-rebuilding-detroit-with-syrian-refugees/

Drug abusers who have gone so far down into their own personal oblivions that they need *government clinics* to shoot up are people who have about as much chance at voting right wing again as I have at winning a Stanley Cup with a team of well-trained rabbits. These people are too often political liabilities for the rest of their lives, even if shooting up in a clean, safe clinic kept them from using dirty needles.

Destroy your brain with drugs, get subsidized to kick the habit by the government, and then feel a mild sense of regret and indebtedness for the rest of your life that results in you watching with a gnawing, vacant dismay as Chinese and Muslims take over your society? Yay! Vote for the Left!

Drug testing for voters? Unthinkable!

-Early childhood education: Every child deserves the chance to live up to his or her God-given potential.

The government is God to the leftists. Get em' into the school system as young as possible so they learn that whites are evil, Harriet Tubman did more for America than Andrew Jackson, and World War II was the Good War. Hillary would love to indoctrinate as many children as she could get her hands on, whole villages of them!

The issues on Crooked Hillary's website go on and on and they all share the same, tired theme of "Government can save the little guy from the rich guy!" Nobody is buying it anymore. Americans are waking up to the small-minded thinking of leftism. We don't need to be taken care of. We require government getting out of the way so we can fulfill our potential.

The political mantras that worked so well in the 1990's and 2000's fall flat today. LGBTs have all the rights they need. Children are getting enough education. Too much, in fact. Drug addicts need jobs, not safe spaces. The moderately wealthy have been bled dry by the super wealthy and their hordes of third world laborers.

Leftism is pathetic. It turns proud, larger than life figures and twists them over the generations into crybullies, dependents, weaklings, addicts, and deviants. Leftism makes people disappear into nothingness while the state's open maw devours everything in sight.

Perspectives: Squatting Slav
twitter.com/squattingslavtv
https://www.youtube.com/channel/UCpfOW3vhZbPMsPHa
8TGjL1Q/

Squatting Slav is best known for his popular, 200k+ subscriber YouTube channel where he conducts "man on the street" style interviews in urban Canada.

-What have you learned from interviewing people on the streets of Canada?

Interviewing protesters on the streets has taught me that most social justice warriors lack very basic factual knowledge surrounding the issues that they are protesting. These people are very easily agitated without any kind of real provocation, and will avoid conversation and arguments at all cost. If they feel they've lost an argument they will usually resort to ad hominem attacks or cheap labels, and their goal at all times seems to be the preservation of what they believe is their moral high ground.

Typically most people I've interviewed are white college students who seem to be in a zombie-like state where the open mindedness and tolerance that they preach about is non-existent.

-Why is your YouTube channel successful?

I believe that my YouTube channel became successful because it came about at a time when anti-social justice warrior videos were huge (during the pre/post Trump election era). I basically filled the vacuum by using a stereotypical Eastern European alpha male character to tease triggered leftists who were already on edge over Russian interference during the elections.

Hearing an Eastern European accent from a tall guy with dark shades definitely invoked a specific kind of reaction from them, which just happened to make for a good video formula. Blending humor with politics has also proven to be a great way of getting the message across to people, especially on topics that are oftentimes heavy or hard to swallow. On top of that I really try to keep my channel content very open and will say whatever I feel without fearing the repercussions.

-If you could change one thing about current Canadian society, what would it be?

If I could change one thing about Canadian society, it would be the current state of political correctness that the country is plagued by. The Trudeau government and liberals are doing everything in their power to censor free speech in Canada and this is leading the country in a very dangerous direction.

Resisting Divide And Conquer

"Divide and rule, the politician cries; unite and lead, is watchword of the wise."

-Johann Wolfgang von Goethe

The world's power elite have known for eons that the most effective way of bringing disparate groups under their central control is to divide them up as much as possible and pit them against each other. This is as much true today as in the days of Rome.

Before the Lyndon Johnson presidency there existed in the United States some semblance of racial courtesy. Things worked at a dysfunctional level. The savage effects of the 1965 Immigration Act and the Johnson administration's practice of putting as many blacks on as much welfare as possible began the generations-long descent into racial discord that has been a blight upon the American public. Decades of failed government policy later, Obama's presidency looked to be the set up for Hillary's final nail in the coffin of race relations.

There is little "ebony and ivory" now that a third of Mexico's population now resides in the USA. A Hillary Clinton administration would have dumped several million Muslims into the USA, igniting a racial powder keg. It's easy to speculate that there would have been ethnic street battles and renegade police districts let feral by the federal agencies themselves infested with an array of internal problems.

The Donald J. Trump administration is a middle finger to the power elite who have divided and conquered us for so long. With the Internet, we have a chance to resist divide and conquer strategies. It is not going to be easy, given how multiculturalism has fragmented America. Radical egalitarianism and welfare-for-all remains the culture of the land. Yet, we still have a chance.

As one of the primary means of resisting divide and conquer, it is of vital importance to undo the globalist brainwashing done upon minorities in the USA. At this point, a "to hell with you" attitude toward minorities is only politically tenable with respect to illegal aliens and Muslims in today's America. Everyone sort of "gets it" that these groups are not and can never truly be a part of the American experiment in freedom.

To resist divide and conquer we need blacks telling other blacks that they don't have to be Democrats and can think for themselves, as Kanye West has so famously done.

To resist divide and conquer we need Latinos recognizing that bringing in Muslims would only further disenfranchise them from participation in the middle class.

We need Jewish people to speak out against the imperialist foreign policy their ultra-rich lobby seeks to sacrifice the lives of American servicemen and women for.

We need gays to speak out against the voyeurism and pedophilia gripping their communities. Gays used to want to integrate into society and be of some use to the broader community. The Democrats and their financiers have emboldened the most corrupt in the LGBT ranks into becoming social activists who want to take over the world.

This is an "all hands on deck" battle against leftism. With people policing their own ranks, society will begin to move away from globalism. Even the most hard core black nationalists[76] and white nationalists seem to be understanding that some measure of cooperation between them is necessary. This does not necessitate integration, particularly of the forced, government variety. It simply means that the blacks will regulate the blacks. Whites will regulate the whites. Jews will regulate the Jews, so on and so forth.

Our alternative is to bicker amongst ourselves as the power elite sell weapons to both sides and profit handsomely. They would use the profits to install a

---

[76]https://www.finalcall.com/artman/publish/Minister_Louis_Farra khan_9/article_105066.shtml

leftist dictator. The world would burn to the ground in the aftermath of the stolen election.

The Danger of Purity Spiraling

A fun thing happens when you begin figuring out principles such as the non-aggression principle: you apply them to everything. This is akin to a two year old who learns how to assert themselves by saying "no" and then proceeds to say "no" to everything. Negating everything as a two year old is age-appropriate. Doing it as an adult is not.

As adults we live in society, as all humans are social to one degree or another. In society there is a lot that is unjust, unfair, abusive, sick, twisted, etc. Violence and shades of grey are an everyday part of living under government rule. This doesn't make it right, this is just our social reality.

Given these conditions, we cannot reasonably say that we'll be able to become successful if we go around saying "no" to everything because "muh principles". Yet, people do it all the time.

These people are generally stuck, in some significant sense, at the developmental level of two year olds. Their parents did not let them have their "no's" once upon a time. Can you imagine it? Grown parents fighting with a two year old because the two year old asserted himself over something as simple as not going potty? Yet, this is extremely commonplace. This is the lack of maturity on the part of so many parents in the world.

The person who purity spirals negates what they perceive to be impure or unprincipled even in the face of their own strategic losses. Some examples of the obstinate negation habit of purity spiralers include:

-Voting for Libertarian Party candidate Gary Johnson (who?) because Hillary and Trump were not "principled"

-Remaining convinced the "working class" is "alienated" because they don't own the "means of production" when these workers are surrounded and harangued on all sides by degeneracy and political correctness

-Not having children because you figure you'll abuse them one day (Africa doesn't give two spits, mate!)

-Stumping for anarcho-capitalism because "Trump is a statist!"

-Negating the teachings of Christianity and replacing them with nothing[77]

-Constantly monitoring your Facebook friends for their slightest philosophical misstep so that you can come in with "curiosity" and get "vulnerable"

-Allowing Europe to be reduced to an IED rubble because some "refugee's" massively produced copy of the Quran says they get to do as they please

-Bagging on someone in your in-group over and over when you could be criticizing the out-group

The examples could go on and on but these are some of the more relevant ones to the culture war.

Purity spiraling denotes an extreme incapacity for negotiation. It's the ignorant or idiot parent stooping to the psychological level of a two year old to engage in a power struggle. Living in the world requires us to negotiate to get what we want. We can't simply declare our principles or our edgy statements and expect to get everything. There are depth and nuance to be engaged in. For depth and nuance, we need strategy.

Being strategic does not mean we abandon our principles. It does mean that we recognize we are most often dealing with people who do not share our high-

---

[77]*tips fedora to liberal atheists

mindedness. We will have to strive for results at whatever level we can get them. We are not screeching two year olds who attempt to impose our ego needs onto the world. We are adults who appreciate sophistication, tact, and responsiveness.

Bolsheviks in the 1920's *made* their terrible ideas become the law of the land. They surveyed the conditions of their prospective dominion and adopted tactics and strategy that would conquer. They were empirical. Their ideological heirs continue to use terror to this day. They never engaged in impotent complaining. They got things done and now we live in their world.

The Left is one of the main groups we culture warriors will have to deal with. We will have to use free speech to convert or paralyze as many of them as we can. It's not as simple as running around on the weekend with anarcho-capitalism flags and bellyaching that things aren't the way we want them to be. The opposition will disregard us and go on to form voting blocks that will allow them to hold office in California[78] and other such real-world achievements.

We can't out-baby the biggest babies. We have to contain them and defeat them. We have to use meme

---

[78]http://freebeacon.com/politics/california-state-assembly-passes-law-to-allow-communists-to-work-in-government/

warfare, free speech rallies, and offer a better way for humanity. These tactics and many more require us to keep our thinking fresh and stay on the cutting edge. There will be more tactics to come. We will have to remain open to using them as conditions change. This is the winning strategy.

Hammering someone in your in-group for being incorrect about something isn't a winning strategy. You can write a tweet, message the person privately if you are in their confidence, or make a YouTube video arguing in good faith where you think they are wrong. Anything beyond that and you begin to undermine them. Unless they have decided to outright abandon your in-group by going to the other side, your reputation will suffer. It's not worth expending energy on people you resent or envy.

No one you go after with your *potentially* better ideas is going to be receptive to you if you purity spiral about it and put the group's overall strategy in danger... particularly if the person is higher in the group's hierarchy than you are. To them you will just look like a pathetic edgelord and get blocked or disregarded.

People higher up in the hierarchy will appreciate your good ideas but only if you present them in a manner that is actionable, profitable to the cause, and humble about your own position in the hierarchy. Take the infantile "no, no, no" out of it and you'll find you are much closer to buy-in than the guy who is always right but can't seem to do anything about it.

Perspectives: Ali Alexander

twitter.com/ali

Ali Alexander is a political operative and communications strategist who has personally collaborated with power players such as Donald J. Trump, Andrew Breitbart, Jack Posobiec, and Mike Cernovich.

What does it take to survive in the world of politics and social commentary?

I believe it takes a consistent brand. That may not mean much, but many brands overextend themselves. It's a poor understanding of economics and consumption habits. For example, restaurants cluster together because studies have shown that consumers will actually go out for dinner more frequently when there are more choices. There's share prosperity. Any content brand that believes it's going to take over the entirety of the market or even a demographic hasn't done their market research. What's emerging online is niche brands. I think what ends up surviving is brands with high integrity and authenticity. Provocation, being first to a scoop, and authority will be brand qualities that may be nice, but I believe they'll be increasingly less important. We're in a great time of transition. We live in a federated future.

(Ali has the distinction of being Kanye West's first retweet on Twitter at a time when Kanye was making major waves through the black community's conscience.)

How did you land on Kanye's radar?

Kanye West has a very high IQ and my audience is full of high IQ viewers, readers, and patrons. I've always loved his music. We were probably attracted by God's cosmic plan. It helps that we share some mutual friends, both on the Left and not-so-left that appreciate my work. There are curious souls among the ranks of our oligarchs. I knew he was consuming some of my work, but I didn't need to tell the world. Everyone is a human—we need to get back to that. I'm done with this Information Age and the bastard celebrity worship system.

How can people organize and win the battle against the Establishment going forward?

People need to network. That's our chief call-to-action. Networking will allow the best ideas to rise to the top, police morality, boost morale, and all the things we're looking for. We also need to be prepared for several collapses.

Navigating Disagreement

An important, early lesson for content creators is the idea that disagreement and dissent is useful and often outright good. We are all finding our independent voices as we build up our platforms. Speaking publicly builds up our personal strength as we test ourselves in the market of ideas. Inevitably, people are going to disagree with us. Everyone has their own point of view, however informed or misinformed. It's important to let others air their disagreements with us so that we can be tested against alternate points of view. This is a lesson I learned in part from Ali, when he brought me on his platform after I aired some disagreements with him. Engagement is built when we dialogue with those disagreeing with us or offering a different angle on things. Engagement builds platforms, plain and simple.

The big trap early content creators fall into is that they squash dissent and disagreement out of personal discomfort. This hurts one's platform in a variety of ways. It decreases engagement. Removing dissent disallows others, usually your followers, a chance to rebut another person's disagreements with your content. Removing dissent and disagreement disallows you the chance to offer your own rebuttals. People don't get to see how you handle disagreement and they miss out on seeing what you're made of.

There is a difference between someone engaging you because they disagree versus someone being an abusive jerk. Someone who is being an abusive jerk will engage you personally, not the arguments and evidence. They will assert things about you that aren't true. Someone just called me a "lunatic" and "mentally ill" just before I sat down to write this essay. I clicked on their YouTube profile and lo and behold: no content uploaded. This person had nothing substantive to offer, just poison. I called them out on this bullying behavior. They promptly deleted their original comments. Put up or shut up.

The golden rule I keep in mind for building my platform is if someone doesn't engage you productively, you don't have to respond productively:

Someone comes around name-calling? Ignore them.

Someone engages you with psychologizing statements about your manner of being? They're specks of dust on the radar, nothing.

Someone seems to engage the arguments in good faith but implies in small doses they are superior to you in grasp of the concepts at hand? Let it set and let them deal with their own grandiosity.

Either a person engages you with respect and curiosity or they go to the back of the line. Life is too short to be spent arguing with idiots with huge walls of text over social media. There's a culture war to fight! People either learn from you or they don't. Those who don't learn anything from you have no grounds by which to engage you. They have better things to do and they just aren't aware of it yet.

Disagreement? Disagreement can be enjoyable. It has to be respectful so that one party or the other doesn't dip things into the personal. We get to hash things out, but only if we engage with respect and curiosity. We have to recognize the competence of another person if we are going to add any value to an exchange of ideas with them. People quite often know more than we do! We can interview them and have a bit of a back and forth. It's all good. People will weigh in on the comments section and offer their own point of view. We don't have to be held in the grips of their worldview. We have formed our own and we can stand on our own two feet in this regard.

One of the most pleasing things to come out of disagreement is that we find out that sometimes we're wrong. This is okay. We're not invested in conclusions when we're fighting a culture war or engaging with philosophy. We're trying to get at the truth! Learning you're wrong on some point of argumentation, some principle, or even just a factoid is massively liberating. Of course, at first, this is threatening. Keep going!

There's no need to spin off into isolation because you were shown to be wrong at some point. Nobody likes a quitter. Keep the conversation going and keep learning. I often get checked and corrected on social media. That doesn't stop me from trying to do the right thing and keep learning how to be better. You don't have to let it keep you from advancing, either.

Disagreement makes us strong, as a society. It's better if it's non-aggressive. There will be some who will be more right, more of the time. We don't have to feel envious of them. They're good, that's all. There will be those who will be wrong most of the time. If they're stubborn to admit it, they won't have much success in building platforms... unless they have great sex appeal or are willing to sell their souls.

Personal power rests not in your ability to override disagreements but to meet them when they're fresh and offer coherent and well-reasoned responses. People being assholes deserve banishment back to the swamps they came from until they learn how to play nicely. This is how civilization works.

Sacrifices

To achieve great things, we must be willing to make sacrifices. Winning the culture war is a great endeavor. The sacrifices each of us will have to make are different. By making sacrifices, we signal to those in our in-group that we are serious about victory. Sacrifice refines us and hardens us into the mature adults we need to be in order to ensure the continuation of civilization.

Our out-groups have made sizeable sacrifices in the name of their causes:

-the global elite have sacrificed the lives of millions of citizens across the world to ensure their multinational governmental bodies

-the global elite also routinely sacrifice hundreds of millions of dollars to finance globalist initiatives aimed at destroying national sovereignty and a sense of identity in ethnic Westerners

-Islam routinely sacrifices the lives of "shaheed" (martyr suicide bombers) and children to drum up sympathy with the corrupt media

-the Deep State in Washington D.C. sacrifices the lives of government operatives and informers to continue their drug and human trafficking operations

-liberals, Democrats, and globalists routinely sacrifice the well-being of their constituencies

-immigrants sacrifice their home countries and the safety of their children in order to make the West worse

-Baby Boomers sacrificed the economic and social well-being of future generations so they could have pensions and avoid being labeled "racist"

These aren't virtuous sacrifices. These are sacrifices that involve countless victims. More appropriately, these are crimes. If we are to hold the moral high ground, we will have to make sacrifices that do not involve innocent victims. We must be willing to sacrifice our illusions. There is much we can do within this purview.

Here are some ways the average Millennial or Gen Z person can sacrifice their illusions to contribute to the greater cause of winning the culture war:

-A daily, weekly, bi-weekly, or monthly $4 energy drink habit can be turned into a "donate to an effective culture warrior's platform" habit of a commensurate amount and frequency. Organizations like InfoWars and Freedomainradio sure could use your money.

-That friendship with that one person who is an energy suck could be tossed into the trash. Suddenly you have more energy to speak truth to power and spend time around people who are actually getting results.

-Video games may be fun in doses but there's a frenzied competition playing out in real life that requires complex mastery of more than just your thumbs and spacial awareness.

-Buying a brand new car feels good but getting a used car and putting the extra money to building your platform feels even better. Same idea applies to going to college or not.

-Those success guru books and videos you get into (see Tim Ferris) may excite you, but remember that the out-groups deal in shifty arguments to undermine the West. You are going to need more than Bulletproof Coffee and Enlightened Belly Tea to Make America Great Again.

-That drug you do "only on the weekends" may numb you to your pain for a bit but it makes you a moral weakling. As Julius Evola would put it, "Habitual use of drugs brings a certain psychic disorganization; one should substitute for them the power of attaining analogous states through one's own means."[79]

-Your family may mean the world to you, but every soldier parts from his family when he goes into the trenches. You could use some independent time or time with other good men to sort out your role to play.

-Watching video game reviews on YouTube might give you some clever quips but it also comes at the expense of reading books like *The Decline of the West* or *The Art of the Deal.*

I am not calling for purity. I am saying that if you want to win the culture war, you're going to have to do as countless men have done in ages past and sacrifice for the good of the cause. You can keep doing any of these things so long as you moderate to the degree to which you can remain effective and achieve results in the culture war.

The more you sacrifice your illusions, the more you will be rewarded. Donald Trump sacrificed being able to ride off into the sunset so he could try and save America. Julian Assange sacrificed a life with his family and the ability to go outdoors to give us the truth of the

---

[79]Evola, Julius. Ride the Tiger: A Survival Manual for the Aristocrats of the Soul. Inner Traditions, 2003.

corrupt power elite. Some men, like Seth Rich, sacrificed their lives.

We all have a choice to sacrifice at whatever level we want. We all have moments in time where our measure as culture warriors is tested. We either give up our illusions and achieve greater results or we shrink from the moment and become embittered and withdrawn.

Practice building the muscle of sacrifice now so that when your moments come you will be ready.

Ode to Ann Coulter

Ann Coulter is one of the most important authors and right wing figures in modern history. As of early 2018, she is a 12 time best-seller. She was raised in a conservative household in Connecticut by John "Jack" Coulter, an FBI agent who hunted Communists and loved Joseph McCarthy. She studied at Cornell and then the University of Michigan. After earning her J.D. in 1988, she spent the majority of the 1990's working in law. Her first book was published by Regnery Publishing in 1998 and she has been in the public eye ever since.

Ann Coulter is important to the right wing for her brash, polemical style that is in short supply. She represents the kind of frontierswoman who was unafraid of drawing a bead on marauding Indians. She is well known for going on the *Stossel Show* and calling libertarians "pussies" (a well-earned moniker). She is also known for going on globalist Jorge Ramos' show and refused to hug an obese illegal alien when pressed to. There was also that time she went on *Father Albert: Hot Under The Collar* and rebuffed screeching insult after screeching insult from a pack of outraged single mothers.

Perhaps most famously, there was that time she was on Bill Maher's show in June 2015 and predicted that, of the declared Republican candidates, Donald Trump had the best chance of winning the general election. Maher's audience and guests howled with laughter and disbelief as Ann sat there unmoved by their raucous derision. Flash forward to November 10th, 2017 and Trump declaring victory in the general election...

Feminists should be bowing at the Altar of Ann. She is exactly the kind of firebrand fighter feminists pretend to champion. Of course, she is not an obese Latina with an attitude, demanding for more Planned Parenthood funding, and thus not worthy of feminist praise. But right wing women can take a play or two out of Ann's book.

She is tough as nails and fierce as a pissed off tiger to her out-groups, most often migrant hordes from the third world and liberal traitors. She is also hip to the racial huckstering of race baiters like Al Sharpton. She does not apologize or cuck in the face of relentless scrutiny, derision, and outright verbal abuse from her critics and haters. She dresses well, makes the most of her looks, and is poised at all times during all media appearances. She is remarkably well-educated, erudite, and well read. She does not prostrate herself before organized globalism.

She does not spare her enemies her mean-spirited quips, precision guided to the most vulnerable spots of hypocrisy in their intellectual armors.

The West needs more women like Ann Coulter. It's a shame she didn't have children, one of the few issues I take with her. However, even stay-at-home mothers can find five minutes here or five minutes there to practice her intense, mother bear instincts. Ann Coulter is the mother of America. She is the crown jewel, the finest of our female intellectuals. She is fighting for the very soul of this nation. She will not cede it to the roving bands of coolies and high level financiers seeking to destroy it from within.

Since she has public, demonstrable influence with President Donald Trump, her current role appears to be to hound and harangue the President when he strays off course from his campaign promises. She is in a high position where her harangues serve a strategic purpose. Exceedingly few others get to claim this privilege. She has earned the right to have "profanity laden shouting matches" with the President[80]. He does seem to eventually come around to her moral guidance but his hands are much more tied on domestic policy than foreign policy.

Time will tell what role Ann Coulter plays in the culture war but look to her as the ideal model for women in the fight.

Meme Warfare and Reality Testing

Knowledge of psychology without knowledge of philosophy basically turns you into a noodling guitarist at a New Age folk festival in the woods of Northern California. Knowledge of philosophy without knowledge of psychology turns you into IBM's

---

[80]http://thegatewaypundit.com/2018/03/report-ann-coulter-potus-trump-had-profanity-laced-shouting-match-in-oval-office/

DeepBlue if a team of Ayn Rand clones were in charge of the programming. It is all too easy to fall too far into one at the expense of the other.

Knowledge of both psychology and philosophy in combination grants you an edge over the out-groups. Most out-groups only have a version of psychology in their repertoire and remain largely ignorant of philosophy:

The Left has psychology down pat but their best and brightest noodle away in the woods.

The Deep State is empowered with the psychological knowledge of how to break a mind.

Hollywood has the psychological knowledge to promote degeneracy and multiculturalism.

Baby Boomers have enough psychological knowledge to exert pressure on their children to go to college and get in massive debt.

The global elite has a superiority complex and more money than the rest of us combined.

Basically no one who opposes Western Civilization has philosophy. Read a few of my books and the source books listed in them, consume a thousand or so Freedomainradio podcasts/videos, read some Nietzsche and Evola, and prepare to blow out the opposition.

Memes are the means of giving others some reality testing. Memes are most often visual representations of emotional states and philosophical principles that the enemies of civilization would prefer be kept hidden. The best memes get you thinking and feeling. Memes are now evolving past images and captions. People are encoding their personalities in a manner that makes them memetic, catchy, and punchy against the opposition. People such as Alex Jones are living, breathing memes. They belong to civilization. This is most effectively done through the study of philosophy.

The Left, my shorthand for the entire group of those opposing or undermining Western Civilization, has understood for decades and decades that appeals to emotion are effective at garnering consent. Think of all the propaganda that was used to convince a peaceful American populace to go into the first World War. Or consider all of the propaganda used in Soviet Russia to convince man to turn in his fellow man to the thought police. Appeals to emotion work. Ask any advertiser, marketing specialist, or public speaker. We live in the public relations age. Psychology is king.

Everyone who is seeking to undermine civilization is using appeals to emotion. We can't hold higher standards and say we are being "principled" by leaving appeals to emotion out of our works. That is suicidal. We have to get with the program.

The major difference between us and the society-wreckers is that our appeals can be based in rationally consistent philosophical principles that encourage people to think for themselves. We help people *break out* of the Matrix. The Left merely convinces people to love the chains that bind them.

A meme or a tweet with just the right balance of psychology and philosophy will blow out of the water any meme that is simply emotional in nature. Plain and simple. The Left can't meme because they do not have the epistemology to unplug people from the Matrix. The Left isn't funny or cutting edge anymore.

There are millions of people out there still suffering from an emotional retreat from reality. They have retreated because of subpar parents who also bought the myths of the ruling class and the Left wholesale. They have retreated because public school ruined their brains. They have retreated because actually dealing with problems in reality is challenging and painful. It's our job to bust them out of prison so they can start to live real lives.

We get to be better at appeals to emotion. The Left only has limp sentimentalism. That's not going to cut it for them and they're finding out real quickly how far behind they are. The Internet is *our* wheelhouse. *We* control "the memes of production".

Time to start churning out the memes. Everyone can meme. Become a meme! Do exciting things with your life and take the piss out of the Establishment. We don't need permission from governments and universities to post in public places. We have unparalleled freedom of speech on the Internet.

One of my favorite memes unfolds comic book style in two panels. In the first panel is an image of a grown man holding his millennial son on his shoulders. They're happy in a glorious, natural scene. The second panel says "20 years later" and shows that boy, all grown up now, and sitting on a bed holding a handgun with a look of extreme rage in his crying eyes. Outside is a parade of LGBT anarcho-communist types, clearly in charge of the society he was once set to inherit. This meme "awakens the Saxon". It reminds us that our society once held a promise. It makes us feel homesick for the America that never came to be. Here's a meme similar to the one I've described:

Thanks to Wikileaks, we know the CIA has tried their hand at memes and is terrible at it[81]. Memes only really work if their creators are moral, empathetic people. We've got em' on the ropes, people. Pour on the memes!

The Dark Malaise

"It is easy for many in the freedom movement to slip into a dark malaise from imbibing the endless toxicity served up by the media. It is important to remember that you have massive control over your life, career, relationships and decisions. Build your own personal paradise."

-Stefan Molyneux

---

[81]http://rare.us/rare-humor/thanks-to-wikileaks-we-now-know-that-the-cia-spends-a-lot-of-time-making-terrible-memes/

As my writing for this book begins to draw to a close, it's a real treat that Stefan tweeted this out earlier in the day. I didn't quite have the term I needed for what he calls a "dark malaise". I referred to it as "war weariness" or "battle fatigue" but it didn't ring like I needed it to.

From my discussions with scores of people participating in the culture war, the dark malaise is a nagging low mood tinged with feelings of helplessness, cynicism, sarcasm, frustration, and bitterness. Moods can be transmitted like diseases. This dark malaise is actually the waking level of consciousness for everyone who is corrupt and working in the mainstream media. These are genuinely unhappy people and they infect everyone who imbibes their toxicity. Even the best of us succumb to the poison pill once in a while. We are, after all, human.

I have endlessly emphasized the concept of boundaries on my YouTube channel and in my previous book, *Make Self-Knowledge Great Again*[82]. Boundaries are standards and dividing lines between us and others. With good boundaries we are able to construct a life of positivity, health, and happiness.

---

[82]http://a.co/1M1wtes

With porous boundaries, we are held hostage by the bigotries and toxicity of whomever we encounter most often... these people serving as representations of the ways we are unable to set limits with ourselves.

For some people, they encounter the mainstream media most often. This is because they forgo in-person connections, career advancement, and family by spending great swaths of time on their devices and televisions. This is the standard mindset and disposition of a person who went through public schooling, passively swallowed down tons of propaganda as their schools became more multicultural, and learned that complaining to authorities got social issues "resolved".

We need to peel this conditioning back by remembering we are not slaves to a system. We must remember what we are fighting for. We are not the media personalities who have compromised their souls in order to serve the dark lords of finance and world government. We are freedom seekers who love our people.

To pull yourself out of the dark malaise, you have to regulate for yourself the stream of information NBC, CNN, Fox News, ABC, and others spew forth. They lie to you, one way or another. Once you've established boundaries that work for you, remember to find something that brings you happiness. Some people go for walks. Some people practice a skill. Some people treat their careers as situations where they can "level up". Some people go on dates or schedule hangouts with friends. Some people talk about current events as a way of getting things off their minds.

Whatever it is, it is in our personal lives where we have the most control. We cannot stop Rachel Maddow from being a globalist propagandist. We cannot perform a citizen's arrest on George Soros...yet. We are hard pressed to stop our local congressman from being a shill and having a bunch of journalists pile lies on top of the shilling. We *can* control the decisions we make in our personal lives. And certainly, we must exert as much influence in the public sphere as we can.

Self-knowledge is the process of discovering our personalities, memories, talents, proclivities, distastes, and capacity to be more human, nobler. While it may not be as sexy as scoring a zinger against a Huffington Post reporter over Twitter, it's downright useful to sometimes simply sit and relax in self-reflection. Who am I? Who am I becoming? What do I feel and why? Why am I pursuing the things in life that I am? How do the people around me influence me?

This kind of proactive living will pull you right out of the dark malaise. Clearly there's a dirty job to be done: drain the swamp. We don't get to just float away to our ivory towers as the world burns. But neither should we dig so far down in the dirt that we become pigs rolling in the muck and loving it. There's a golden mean. The Stefan Molyneux tweet I quoted earlier and his powerful speech at A Night For Freedom[83] serve to remind us that we need to bear in mind what we are fighting for, lest we become the thing we're fighting against.

Dudes Who Argue Against Their Own Existence

Many are sick of tribalism; many are just getting into it. Regardless of our personal feelings on it, tribalism is a part of reality. It is here to stay. No amount of high philosophizing will ever defeat the basic, biological fact of reality that people who share characteristics will tend to associate accordingly. These associations form societies.

Contrary to popular, ivory tower academic notions, tribalism and individualism are not necessarily at odds. The most radical individualist benefits from

[83]https://youtu.be/Yc3z06unwWI

electricity, plumbing, food supply, and waste disposal systems. The quality of these services is determined by the organizational coherence of the businesses offering them. These businesses, particularly in the West, have almost exclusively been formed by straight, white men who identified with one another. Businesses that are multicultural are more likely to fail when stacked against homogenous groups or groups with a homogenous elite making the decisions. It is no surprise that most dedicated individualists make their careers in Western nations wherein all of the wealth and positive economic momentum has been established primarily by high IQ, straight white males.

Healthy individualism is all about the romantic vision of a man who stands against the mob for higher moral standards and a more truthful society.

Many prominent individualists cling to the basic stance of this romantic vision, man against the mob, and forget about the truth value of their arguments and whether this is a false dichotomy or not. They forget to reality test.

For example, an individualist may be ignorant of demographics and assume that low IQ, non-Westerners can eventually integrate into the West and effect all of the cultural, economic, and social splendor that has been a part of the Western tradition in the past. Just give those third worlders a journaling course to improve their collegiate outcomes! This person, attached as they are to the image of the man against the mob, will choose as his target a large group of people opposed to immigration into the West. He will pester them with his appeals to remember that people must be judged as individuals. The true individualists in this equation are the ones who are willing to preserve the higher standards of the West by not allowing non-Westerners in.

Those opposed to non-Western immigration understand that you can't expect a functioning society to form by lumping in all the individualists of all the different races into one country together and expect the historical success of the West to continue unabated. This will simply result in a massive brain drain out of the third world. High-minded, individualist, recent émigrés will, regardless, have economic incentives to divert resources out of the first world into the third world. These resources will evaporate because the local populations in the third world will not have the discerning individualists they once had to ensure their proper utilization. The first world will eventually be impoverished and race relations will sicken as the size of government balloons to try and get as many people on welfare as possible.

One particularly slick talking point against tribalism is the choice, unconscious or conscious, on the part of "noble" individualists to focus on the tribalism of the majority in the West and none else. These individualists use the technological innovations brought about by traditionally straight white males to argue against straight white male societal cohesion. Those who *are* straight white males who choose to argue against straight white male cohesion are a special kind of destructive, whether they know it or not. They deliver the children and wives of these straight white males to hordes of rapists, murderers, child molesters, and so forth, since non-Western standards for the treatment of children and women are abysmal, Japan aside. These people should be confronted on their incomplete, non-empirical arguments. They paralyze cohesive, in-group efforts on the part of straight white males to ensure their posterity and civilizational continuity. These manipulators show with their indignation that since they're debilitating their own in-group in the name of something noble, an outdated version of individualism, they're not culpable for the scorn and ostracism heaped upon them when they do not respond to fair rebuttals.

The way out of this mind trap is to embrace the idea that individuals can come together through identifying as hailing from a tradition of individualism in order to work together to identify those who do not come from said tradition.

Cynicism and the Shame Brigade

"Cynical" is defined as:

1. distrusting or disparaging the motives of others; like or characteristic of a cynic.

2. showing contempt for accepted standards of honesty or morality by one's actions, especially by actions that exploit the scruples of others.

3. bitterly or sneeringly distrustful, contemptuous, or pessimistic.

There's lots of infighting in nationalist and right wing movements and much of it is characterized by cynicism. Someone, most often a person who fancies themselves as some sort of purist, will engage cynicism into the social space by disparaging the motives of another. A big brouhaha develops wherein everyone who has not processed their own cynicism will join sides either in the attack on the person with supposedly less-than-savory motives or in the defense of the person to clear their name. Only the few who have resolved their own cynicism will look at the initiating offense: speculation of another person's motives and feigned certainty.

To know another person's motives, you ask them. Otherwise, you can only speculate and piece together narratives based on a person's actions. When you engage in this speculation publicly, you encourage others to develop their own theories. This is a slippery slope as it signals to out-groups that there's social utility to publicly speculating on the internal states of a member of your in-group. The resulting "certainty" that people stake their reputations on is where the problem really develops.

Until a person's motivations are directly queried, and that's a big "if" since most people are not at ease and trusting when they feel they've come under personal scrutiny, the fact remains that motives have not been established beyond the shadow of a doubt. Yet, so many want to prance about like they have absolute certainty. It's a sticky trap to avoid feeling your own uncertainty by pretending certainty. The lower the IQ of people engaged in this, the more brutish and mob-like the resulting social circumstances become.

Cynicism is an infectious disease, particularly in the social media age. Whole witch hunts are organized because some cynical person suspects "bad motives" and "insincerity" in another person. Those leading the hunts launch themselves into campaigns of false certainty, often resorting to slander and outright lies, in order to establish that the target has unhealthy psychological processes. All this drama and so little progress.

It takes a bigger person to ask oneself, "Why am I so invested in establishing that this other person has bad motives?" The self-reflection usually doesn't come, but let's hope this essay catalyzes some.

Bad behavior is more easily tracked and labeled. That's not enough for the cynic. He has to establish bad motives. Once this is established, through false certainty, no steps at remediation of the offender have to be taken. He has no willingness to grant qualifiers to the person he is criticizing. No curiosity as to the variety and scope of the target's motives must be engaged since, after all, the motives were unequivocally bad! Why? Because a cynical person had a hunch! How convenient.

This may come as a shocker to some: there are people in the world who have done degenerate, unhealthy, dishonest, or outright immoral things who, if approached with curiosity, will begin to see the error in their ways.

The hang up is that cynical people generally don't engage in curiosity as a means of resolving conflict.

People who are attacked with false certainty don't readily yield to any reasonable argumentation embedded within that false certainty attack. Why justify oneself to cynical people? This establishes the standard that any traumatized knucklehead who intellectually identifies you as having done something socially unproductive in your life is therefore entitled to speculate, with full certainty, on your inner experiences and attack you how he sees fit. You have to take it since, after all, you were bad and need a good scolding. Suddenly people with the social skills of a bridge troll can just bludgeon any misbehavior in others with cynicism. What a big happy family!

Those who are self-respecting know that they have the freedom to make mistakes and even be wrong sometimes without the Shame Brigade coming by and setting up a permanent encampment. To self-respecting people, the Shame Brigade just looks like a motley crew of cynical people with crippling perfectionism. They are toxic. In an age where we have instant social access to others via public profiles, these people feel entitled to "regulate" on members of their own in-group with nary a thought as to the possibility that perhaps this offender has already chosen a path to reformation, however difficult to perceive. No self-respecting person needs someone else jumping down their throat. It's simply not a part of civil discourse. Appeals to self-knowledge, however, are a part of civil discourse. Receiving criticism and addressing it publicly is a responsibility when you are influential.

Since, in this cynical worldview, there is no standard for personal improvement or even the slightest idea of how that actually works, there can be no improvement for the target that allows them to soar to greater heights. Instead, they must be ground underfoot by the Shame Brigade. Only when they have the social standing of dirt will they be allowed to whimper publicly from time to time about some insignificant detail. Fortunately, there are enough good people in place to fight back the mob and ensure that those who wish to self-rehabilitate are allowed the space and encouragement to do it.

The Shame Brigade is not interested in prevention as a social measure other than to string up targets and leave their corpses as cautionary tales to others. They do not have the social skills to engage someone at a personal level, discover their aspirations for life, and assertively point out the incongruity between a course of action they're set to endeavor upon and a virtuous life.

By and large, this is simply an analogy for how children are taught and encouraged to improve or be punished into submission to go join the mob in public school.

Winners and Losers, Closers and Quitters

"Coach Steele: Rudy, are you ready for this, champ?
Rudy: I've been ready for this my whole life!
Coach Steele: Then you take us out on the field."

-from the film Rudy

"John Mason: Your "best"?! Losers always whine about their best. Winners go home and fuck the prom queen.
Stanley Goodspeed: Carla was the prom queen.
John Mason: Really?
Stanley Goodspeed: [cocks his gun] Yeah."

-from the film The Rock

"Nobody likes a quitter" is a phrase used at a couple points in this book. It's a truism. There's a special enmity we hold in the West for quitters. Perhaps it comes out of the story of Judas Iscariot quitting on Jesus and then selling him out to the Jewish priest class. Wherever it comes from, revulsion for the quitter is a winning group strategy. Quitting is a losing strategy.

A quitter is a person who comes to be depended on by a group for their abilities. Rather than gradually fade out their involvement or declare far in advance their choice to retire from competition, the quitter leaves suddenly. They burn their bridges. Often it is in a fit of self-righteousness but probably just as often it is done as a coward slinking away from challenges too great for their own personal reckoning.

Quitters don't have heart. They are not people of personal strength. You can often pick out a quitter just by looking at their body. Is there a sickliness to them? Do they have man boobs? Are they obese? Do they play a lot of video games? They're probably going to quit on you. Steer clear and save yourself the trouble. Once it's time for the rubber to meet the road and they have to stake personal pain or gain for the next advance to happen, their heart just isn't in it. Their hearts are weak.

Losers are perpetual quitters. Quitting poisons a person's constitution. Poison it enough and there begins to be downward momentum. Only the quitter can shake themselves out from the losing streak. The more of a loser they become, the greater the risk they're going to have to take to break the spell.

Real risk comes from combatting the out-group. Parroting the leaders of the in-group, while helpful, involves no real risk. It's much easier to disappear as a follower in the aftermath of a lost battle than it is to disappear if you're a bonafide leader. No, to redeem himself the quitter must take honest-to-God risks out on the battlefield against the out-group.

Parroting the leaders of the in-group will garner you some attention. You will eventually be called upon to perform a higher responsibility for the in-group. There are extremely few valid excuses for not stepping it up to the next level. Yet, so many weak men and women back out when this time comes. They prefer their quiet lives of desperation and isolation.

You can anticipate a quitter by some of the following signs:

-has a loose sense of time with respect (disrespect) to appointments

-complains

-manages the expectations of those around them

-man boobs, obesity, sickliness, use of soy products

-in monetary debt they can't pay back

-prefers Facebook over Twitter or YouTube

-never played organized sports growing up

-no social life

-perpetual dating woes

-no children

-all brains, no heart

-doesn't actually combat the out-group, just white-knights for the in-group leaders against other in-group members

-talks big talk coming into a situation and doesn't back it up

-isn't bothered by losses

-criticizes people who have created value when they haven't created any value

-slinks away from conflicts they started

-flakey, doesn't show up when they say they will

-avoids winners out of envy

Quitters and losers will sink any organization. These people aren't willing to do whatever it takes to accomplish the mission at hand. They are forever reenacting how their own parents backed out or dropped out on some important endeavor that was originally mutually committed to. Quitters are the parent who doesn't get their daughter a pony like they promised to. Quitters are the dad that doesn't show up to son's baseball game or a weekend visitation. Quitters are the mother who divorced her husband because she thought she'd try to upgrade before hitting her biological wall.

Winners have heart. Literally, their hearts are strong. Figuratively, blood pumps through their veins. They're everything quitters and losers avoid having to be. Winners love responsibility. Winners are closers. They don't give up on the mission until it's seen through. Winners show up. They take it to the out-group with real risks out on the battlefield.

In the same way that perpetual quitters become losers, perpetual closers become winners. Here are some identifiers of winners:

-stick to appointment times and reschedule only once in a while with fair notice and good reason

-strong, hearty physique that is desirable to the opposite
sex

-in the black financially, runs their own business

-fights out in the open on Twitter and YouTube

-played organized sports growing up and attained an
accolade or even a championship

-understands the roots of their complaints and
addresses problems at their source rather than airing
unprocessed crap

-engaging, varied social life

-success with the opposite sex culminating in marriage
and children

-brains and heart but *at least* heart (you can't help
having brains or not but you *can* help having heart)

-combats the out-group and addresses in-group issues
only as a means of taking on more responsibility

-rather than big talk, comes in soberly and addresses the
situation with an aim to win, win, win

-takes losses personally and then gets back on the horse
to ride some more

-stakes their own creative works against whomever's
they are critiquing

-doesn't start conflicts but finishes them

-never sells out his fellow man, ever

-shows up

-filter out losers/quitters out of meritocratic self-preservation

Revulsion for the quitter is a winning group strategy because the quitter drags down others with them. This type of behavior is undesirable and anti-civilizational. Children are much more immune from criticism for quitting because they are still learning and dependent on their parents, which is a luck of the dice situation. Adults have to engage society as independents and it is on them that we place responsibility, to the degree the competition mattered at the highest philosophical levels.

Adulation for the winner is also a winning group strategy, granted whatever they won at actually advances civilization. George W. Bush may have had a "Mission Accomplished" banner flying on the USS Abraham Lincoln in 2003 for having defeated Iraq but in truth it was a globalist war that did absolutely nothing for the average American. America was Bush's supposed team. Donald J. Trump winning the presidency *actually* meant something because he has gone on to ease restrictions on coal miners and pull

America out of the disastrous Trans-Pacific Partnership agreement. He has also brokered peace negotiations between North and South Korea and put a constitutionalist on the Supreme Court. When he was fighting at a lower philosophical level, for The Trump Organization, he was a winner for his employees. You could even say Trump was bred to win, from good genes.

We can be winners in the culture war, but we have to shed the losers from our ranks and neutralize the loser tendencies within ourselves. We have to show up, fight with real heart, and close the deal. We didn't start the culture war but we will end it.

Resources

Adams, Scott. *Win Bigly: Persuasion in a World Where Facts Don't Matter.* Portfolio HC, 2017.

Byrne, Gary J., and Grant M. Schmidt. *Crisis of Character: a White House Secret Service Officer Discloses His Firsthand Experience with Hillary, Bill, and How They Operate.* Center Street, 2017.

Bawer, Bruce. *While Europe Slept: How Radical Islam Is Destroying the West from Within.* Anchor Books, 2007.

Conservative, Anonymous. *The Evolutionary Psychology behind Politics: How Conservatism and Liberalism Evolved within Humans.* Federalist Publications, 2012.

Coulter, Ann. *In Trump We Trust: E Pluribus Awesome!* Sentinel, 2016.

Donovan, Jack (University of York, UK). *Becoming a Barbarian.* Dissonant Hum, 2016.

Evola, Julius. *Ride the Tiger: A Survival Manual for the Aristocrats of the Soul.* Inner Traditions, 2003.

Fallaci, Oriana. *The Force of Reason.* Rizzoli, 2006.

Greer, Scott. *No Campus for White Men: the Transformation of Higher Education into Hateful Indoctrination.* WND Books, Incorporated, 2017.

Molyneux, Stefan. *The Art of the Argument: Western Civilization's Last Stand*. Stefan Molyneux, 2017.

Pressfield, Steven. *Gates of Fire: An Epic Novel of the Battle of Thermopylae*. Bantam Books, 2005.

Putnam, Robert D. *Bowling Alone: The Collapse and Revival of American Community*. Simon & Schuster, 2007.

Raspail, Jean. *The Camp of the Saints*. The Social Contract Press, 1994.

Salatin, Joel. *Folks, This Ain't Normal*. Center Street, 2012.

Scott, Ridley, director. *Blade Runner - The Final Cut*. 2007.

Southern, Lauren. *Barbarians: How Baby Boomers, Immigrants and Islam Screwed My Generation*. Rebel News Network, 2016.

Trump, Donald J. *Crippled America: How to Make America Great Again*. Threshold Editions, 2016.

Trump, Donald, and Tony Schwartz. *Trump the Art of the Deal*. Ballantine Books, 2017.

Tzu, Sun. *The Art of War*. Greyhound Press, 2017.

Made in the USA
Monee, IL
26 November 2020